The Manager: a poem

Selected Writings 2

RICHARD BERENGARTEN was born in London in 1943, into a family of musicians. He has lived in Italy, Greece, the USA and former Yugoslavia. His perspectives as a poet combine English, French, Mediterranean, Jewish, Slavic, American and Oriental influences.

Under the name RICHARD BURNS, he has published more than 25 books. In the 1970s, he founded and ran the international Cambridge Poetry Festival. He has received the Eric Gregory Award, the Wingate-Jewish Quarterly Award for Poetry, the Keats Poetry Prize, the Yeats Club Prize, the international Morava Charter Poetry Prize and the Great Lesson Award (Serbia). He has been Writer-in-Residence at the international Eliot-Dante Colloquium in Florence, Arts Council Writer-in-Residence at the Victoria Centre in Gravesend, Royal Literary Fund Fellow at Newnham College, Cambridge, and a Royal Literary Fund Project Fellow. He has been Visiting Associate Professor at the University of Notre Dame and British Council Lecturer in Belgrade, first at the Centre for Foreign Languages and then at the Philological Faculty. He is currently a Bye-Fellow at Downing College, Cambridge, and Praeceptor at Corpus Christi College, Cambridge. His poems have been translated into more than 90 languages.

By Richard Berengarten

THE SELECTED WRITINGS OF RICHARD BERENGARTEN
   Vol. 1 *For the Living: Selected Longer Poems, 1965–2000*
   Vol. 2 *The Manager*
   Vol. 3 *The Blue Butterfly*   (*The Balkan Trilogy*, Part 1)
   Vol. 4 *In a Time of Drought* (*The Balkan Trilogy*, Part 2)
   Vol. 5 *Under Balkan Light* (*The Balkan Trilogy*, Part 3)

POETRY (WRITTEN AS RICHARD BURNS)
   The Easter Rising 1967
   The Return of Lazarus
   Double Flute
   Avebury
   Inhabitable Space
   Angels
   Some Poems, Illuminated by Frances Richards
   Learning to Talk
   Tree
   Roots/Routes
   Black Light
   Croft Woods
   Against Perfection
   Book With No Back Cover
   Manual: the first 20
   Holding the Darkness (Manual: the second 20)
   Holding the Sea (Manual: the third 20)

AS EDITOR
   An Octave for Octavio Paz
   Ceri Richards: Drawings to Poems by Dylan Thomas
   Rivers of Life
   In Visible Ink: Selected Poems, Roberto Sanesi 1955–1979
   Homage to Mandelstam
   Out of Yugoslavia
   For Angus
   The Perfect Order: Selected Poems, Nasos Vayenas, 1974–2010

The Manager
a poem

Selected Writings
Volume 2

RICHARD BERENGARTEN

Shearsman Books

Published in the United Kingdom in 2011 by
Shearsman Books Ltd
58 Velwell Road
Exeter
EX4 4LD

Isbn 978 1 84861 176 4

Copyright © Richard Berengarten, 2004, 2008, 2011
All rights reserved.

Preface copyright © Chris Hamilton-Emery, 2008.

The right of Richard Berengarten to be identified as the
author of this work has been asserted by him in accordance
with Section 77 of the Copyright, Designs and Patents Act 1988.

First published in paperback by Elliott & Thompson, London, 2001.
Second, hardcover edition by Salt Publishing, Cambridge, 2008.
This third edition, first published in 2011,
contains some textual corrections.

To Whom It May Concern

Contents

Preface xi
Acknowledgements xix

Under the plane tree an old woman knits   3

PART ONE
1. *Gemini*   7
2. Our evenings together   8
3. Dad I can't get to sleep   9
4. Well Charles what'll it be   10
5. Day invades the curtains   11
6. Dancing half canned at Miriana's party   12
7. I yet myself continually   13
8. How I piss myself off   14
9. *Confidential Memo*   16
10. In tele-sales she said   18
11. It has never been like this   20
12. *Prospectus*   21
13. Hello, she sighs   23
14. October then   24
15. It was love perfect passion   26
16. Boarded the Twin Com   27
17. As a child on the playground edge   28
18. Coming in Wintersfield   30
19. As she stripped   31
20. Am I stealing you from your husband   32
21. Some people you can tell   33
22. One Thursday I skipped school   34

23.	He's a lurcher not a whippet	36
24.	You are a true blue brick Tony	38
25.	Your silence squeezes me dry	39
26.	Am I interrupting you	40
27.	She had a curious way	42
28.	You're pretending again	43
29.	What's a woman like me to do	44
30.	My name? *Homo aspirans*	46
31.	She's watching *The Holocaust*	48
32.	This morning every object	50
33.	Is that the telephone ringing	51
34.	Gasparo Napolitano in fullest flight	52
35.	So that afternoon she flits	54
36.	Yes hello there Looie hello	56
37.	A lecture	58
38.	Tonight she's in bed with her Cypriot	60
39.	Cover me Manoula	62
40.	Now it's autumn	63
41.	Sipping Earl Grey in the Orangerie	64
42.	Far too many years	66
43.	Dozing, half past something	68
44.	Room 1409	70
45.	If I may make so bold as to speak	72
46.	This bed smells of Eleni Deirdre Jane	74
47.	Once in bed you said	75
48.	Well this Adam Kadmon mate	76
49.	My arms have been amputated	78
50.	Hello. Hello. Are you there	80
51.	I sit behind my desk	81

Curriculum Vitae   83

Part Two

52.	Last night I was kept awake	87
53.	Through the aerial arrival gate	88
54.	Why you must to tell me	90
55.	A polythene green dragon	92
56.	The Saturday before they left	93
57.	*Memo. To: Psychometric Testing Evaluation Unit*	94
58.	There go the dead again	96
59.	If I were to speak I'd call up the dead	98
60.	I lift myself from despair	99
61.	And if I were to greet you	100
62.	To say Mummy again	101
63.	Snowfall, two feet, at Green Hedges	102
64.	The car turning the corner	103
65.	I have spent much of my time looking	104
65.	What I have lost is perpetual	105
66.	I have searched all over this house	106
68.	Sir. Since the living	108
69.	Here my darling is the house	110
70.	Chill east wind from Poland	112
71.	Nobody calls	114
72.	The minister has been tainted	115
73.	He chats to me cheerily	116
74.	Adam Kadmon hangs upside down	118
75.	Cedar Ward	120
76.	Damnedness and madness	121
77.	This is a Reassessment Unit	122
78.	*Hip Know sissies*	124
	Hypnosis is	125
79.	*Fax: Urgent*	126
80.	We thought things might get better	128
81.	After betrayal and after bereavement	129
82.	This limestone cavern has the hugest mouth	130
83.	Through heathered acres	131

84.	I have tried to make sense of my life	132
85.	*Email*	134
86.	All the people I need to talk to	135
87.	A hidden agenda	138
88.	When did I last see myself	140
89.	Auntie Mimi has died	142
90.	Oh my cousin	143
91.	Closed the front door quietly	144
92.	I cannot make it cohere	146
93.	To be not here, or anywhere	147
94.	One street on my citymap always eludes me	148
95.	In the parks and among the flowering gardens	150
96.	This is a petition	152
97.	Do not approach	154
98.	The aeon lies torn in pieces	155
99.	I've been trying to get through for ages	156
100.	You who sit waiting for me	157

Noon. A sky of jade   159

Postscript   161
Notes   163

Preface

The Manager is the second volume in the ongoing series of *Selected Writings* by Richard Berengarten. Through its previous publications, under the name Richard Burns, this book-length poem has a curious history. It was first effectively noticed by Barry MacSweeney, who published four sections from it as a work-in-progress in *Poetry South East*, 1980:

> Richard Burns, a poet from Cambridge, is currently working in Gravesend. *The Manager* is a fabulous work. I wish I had room to publish more, or cash to print the lot. Its tense, hysterical edges (no insult) and jagged rhythms are just what we need in the eighties. More and more we need to record the breakdown, anger, frustration, paranoia and downright bloodiness of society. Richard has his writing hand on the thudding pulse. It will make a fine book.[1]

In 1982, this first editorial response was followed up by the leading American journal of postmodern literature, *Boundary 2*, which published thirty sections.[2] Six years later, in 1988, Elaine Feinstein chose three extracts for *PEN New Poetry II*.[3] Reviewing that anthology in *The Guardian*, Carol Ann Duffy wrote:

> Some poets soar above straightforward craftsmanship. [The] extracts from *The Manager* by Richard Burns give a genuine frisson with their stark originality.

In 1987, the author left England to live in Yugoslavia. One unexpected result of his move was that a draft of *The Manager* was published by the Writers' Association of Montenegro in 1990, so the book had the unique distinction of appearing in Serbo-Croatian translation eleven

---

[1] Barry MacSweeney, guest ed., 'Introduction', *Poetry South East* 5, South East Arts, Tunbridge Wells, 1980.
[2] Richard Burns, '30 Extracts from *The Manager*', *Boundary 2*, XII/1, ed. William V. Spanos, State University of New York at Binghamton, pp. 15–31.
[3] Richard Burns, 'Three Extracts from *The Manager*', *P. E.N. New Poetry II*, ed. Elaine Feinstein, Quartet Books, London, 1988, pp. 21–24.

xi

years before its first full appearance in English.[4] Unfortunately, it came out when Yugoslavia was on the verge of falling apart.

By January 1991, Burns had returned to England, and the poet and editor Anthony Rudolf, a good friend of his, showed the English text to the far-sighted London literary agent Giles Gordon. Gordon's response was rapid and unequivocal: 'I suspect, quite genuinely, that *The Manager* may be a masterpiece and posterity will recognise it as such.' But he added: 'Therefore it is extremely feeble of me to say that I don't believe I'd be able to find a publisher for it [. . .] and certainly not next week.'[5]

Giles Gordon's predictions proved right. The poetics of *The Manager* were scarcely in keeping with the post-Thatcherian 1990s. Indeed, the poem is interpretable, at least in part, as an exposé of the hollowness and shallowness of Thatcherism. For all its wit, it is also replete with elements that some readers still find uncomfortable, discomfiting, disturbing. At any rate, a first full English edition was not to appear in print for another ten years, when Anthony Rudolf, a consistently loyal advocate of the book, showed a copy to the London publishing consultant David Elliott, who was immediately enthusiastic. The eventual result was that the firm Elliott and Thompson was founded *because* its editors knew they had to publish *The Manager*. It was their first book, and they took considerable pains in its printing and design. David Elliott's sleeve-notes claimed:

> *The Manager* is a long poem of a new kind. In presenting the reader with fictional episodes from the life of one man, it offers an account of the disjunctions and contradictions of modern-day living. The text bristles with outrage, anger, obsession, loss and romance, interwoven with passages of a wry, sardonic humour. It merges characters, interactions and drama. Its medium, the 'verse-paragraph', enables the reader to capture an impressive range of the registers, inflexions and nuances of contemporary language in all its forms.[6]

---

[4] *Menadžer*, tr. Jasna B. Mišić and Vladimir Sekulić, with introduction by Anthony Rudolf, Udruženje Crne Gore, Titograd, 1990.
[5] Giles Gordon, letter to Richard Burns. January 17, 1991. Text supplied by RB.
[6] David Elliott (unattributed), description on inside front flap, *The Manager, a poem*, 1st edition, Elliott & Thompson, London & Bath, 2001.

But perhaps not surprisingly, with the exemplary exceptions of *Poetry Review* and the *London Magazine*,[7] the mainstream culture managers and fashionable reviewers bypassed the book entirely, wouldn't touch it with a barge pole. London stayed impermeable, unstirred, unmoved.

Even so, as often happens with genuinely new, original and powerful poetry, reception of *The Manager* started to go through a series of slow and gradual drifts. The book began to find its own way and ways, turning up in unexpected peripheries, rooting itself here and there, occupying edges, filling hollows, spilling onto and over ledges. For example, it achieved glistening responses in Swansea (Wales), Plymouth and Exeter (Devon), Athens (Greece), South Bend (Indiana), New Orleans, and Tbilisi (Georgia). From South Wales, poet and critic Jeremy Hooker wrote:

> I find *The Manager* brilliant, a work of sustained brilliance. It is everywhere exceptionally well written, with a linguistic versatility that is rare in any writing and sometimes calls to mind Joyce, not by suggesting a debt to him, but by virtue of its control of language, its knowledge of words. [. . .] The work has immense verbal richness, it delights in words, it knows them intimately, it knows their many diverse use for different purposes, and therefore has a considerable range of voices, a range far wider than *The Waste Land*. [. . .] It is in the voices, above all – romantic, lyrical, sardonic, self-condemned by cliché, 'managerial', 'popular', 'bitter', tender – that *The Manager* at once composes and reveals, projects and diagnoses a whole modern world with its conditions of life. [. . .] I do not know another poem, or indeed any writing, which is at once so expert in our modern consumerist specialist language, and so witty in exposing their superficiality and heartlessness.[8]

From Edinburgh, the historian and poet Angus Calder wrote for *The London Magazine*:

---

[7] 'This is an extremely ambitious and interesting work – one that needs to be read and reread.' Jonathan Treitl, 'From the Ludoslovakian', *Poetry Review*, 92/1, 2002, p. 55. See note 9 below for Angus Calder's review in *The London Magazine*.

[8] Jeremy Hooker, letter to Richard Burns, 2002. Text supplied by RB. See also the same author's review. 'Handling Experience' in *Swansea Review*, 22, 2003, pp. 114–118.

In a cycle of a hundred poems, with three very fine detached lyrics, Burns takes Charles Bruno from cynically philandering middle management through marital and mental breakdown to the point where he speaks as a prophet in the Old Testament sense, winning past death to endorse life. [. . .] Burns has pulled off the rare feat of creating an experimental poem which is at every point wholly accessible. [. . .] It cannot be said that Charles Bruno alias Adam Kadmon alias Cadman is a 'consistent' or 'rounded' character. Which is, I take it, part of Burns' point. Each in his own prison, to bring in Eliot again, experiences himself as multiple. Escaping the prison to face up to our Usness entails not 'rounded' barging but open-eyed dissolution, as far as possible, into the life around us. Well, that's how I'd put it, and I wouldn't have phrased that thought this way if I hadn't been thinking hard about Burns' truly remarkable poem.[9]

Two further comments endorsed Calder's response. The novelist Nicholas Mosley wrote: 'I found *The Manager* intensely powerful and moving – like Dylan Thomas's raging against the dying of the light. It is a savage paean of praise for life. The protagonist becomes a giant figure.'[10] And the critic and journalist Val Hennessy noted: 'I found it absolutely riveting. It is a wrenched-from-the-heart work, packed with good things and zapping along in a very compelling manner.'[11] Similarly, in January 2003, Steve Spence in Plymouth published a rave review on the *Terrible Work* website:

This epic poem sequence [. . .] looks set to become one of the major works of the last part of the 20th century, hovering edgily on the 21st. [. . .] There are a hundred 'poems' which revolve around the life of 'The Manager', a title which hints both at the pervasive nature of late 20th century business culture and the notion of an individual attempting to manage his own life. I guess the work's unifying subject is ultimately the attempt to reconstitute the idea of 'history' from the ravages of postmodernism, both as a political theory and as cultural deprivation, but it's a poem which so abounds with life, with energy and with such a wide array of voices and different regis-

---

[9] Angus Calder, 'A Spectacular Variety of Registers', *The London Magazine*, December/January 2004, pp. 88–94.
[10] Nicholas Mosley, note to RB, 2001. Supplied by RB.
[11] Val Hennessy, note to David Elliott, 2001.

ters that you just have to dip in and go with the flow. It's a poem about people, about society, about breakdown in an age of information overload and business uniformity, that takes on big issues through fragmented narratives which point towards a wider picture. *The Manager* is a work which revels in form, technique and wordplay while never quite losing sight of its objective. It's a poem which has 'heart' at its centre, feeling as its source but which never denies the pleasures of the cerebral in so doing. It's that rare thing, also, a poem 'about' language which nevertheless has the potential to reach a wide audience. Hopefully, that will happen because I think it's also an important statement about the confusions and difficulties of the age we live in from the pen of a writer who is clearly working at the peak of his powers. I suspect this work has been some considerable time in the making and looks like becoming Burns' magnum opus. [. . .] This may well turn out to be the book of the decade. Get hold of a copy and read it. Re-read it.[12]

Then, in summer 2003, a highly successful dramatised version was performed by lead actors from the Royal Shakespeare Company at the 50th Stratford-upon-Avon Poetry Festival. Roger Pringle, director of the Festival, wrote in the programme:

It is well known that a major new artistic or literary work rarely achieves immediate acceptance, let alone acclaim or even recognition. There is often a time-gap before it reaches a wider public. It is almost as though the world offered a natural resistance, which a new work has to challenge and break.

The Manager is a long poem which explores modern experience in a modern idiom. It is a poem of its time and for its time; an expression of our age, and a critique of it. In turn humorously, ironically, even savagely, it examines contemporary behaviour in the business-world, male/female relationships, family life, politics. It is a sequential, connected poem which, like its publishing history, contains elements of surprise and fascinating twists. And because it disregards established poetic norms and creates its own, publishers in Britain did not know what to do with it. Not so, however, in former Yugoslavia. An earlier version of the poem was first published by the Association of Writers of Montenegro in 1990 in a Serbo-Croat

---

[12] Steve Spence, January 2003, http://www.terriblework.co.uk/Archive%20whole.htm, consulted July 17, 2008; no longer accessible.

translation. (At the time the author was living in Serbia.) Eventually, the book was taken on by David Elliott and Brad Thompson, who founded their new firm, Elliott and Thompson, in order to publish it. Their finely designed edition came out quietly in November 2001.

Since then, by word of mouth, around the edges of the poetry world in the UK and abroad, by means of appearances at poetry readings, at festivals and conferences, and among the literary avant-garde as well as among well-known writers, journalists and critics, a slow and steady swell of praise has been growing. It is our belief and hope that the appearance of *The Manager* as the finale to the 50th Stratford-upon-Avon Poetry Festival marks yet another phase in the appreciation and recognition of a major long poem.[13]

Writing from West Point, New York, the American critic Patrick Query comments:

> Virtually every thematic element of the poem is contingent, shifting, negotiable, ungovernable. The form, though, is never negotiable, and from that tension emerges the special genius of the poem; and this is why Burns may be said to have written, against impossible odds, a great poem of hope. [. . .] *The Manager* itself is a kind of provisional answer to some of the most vexing questions about the place of poetry in the contemporary world. [. . .] Despite its strangeness, *The Manager*, one might say, is a thoroughly hospitable poem. [. . .] Yet *The Manager* is about more than managing, more than simply hanging on. It is also about the deliberate search for a meaningful order that includes both life's fractious material and its capacity to support utter beauty and joy.[14]

As is suggested by this brief outline of some of the critical and editorial responses to *The Manager*, in terms of its balancing on peripheries and

---

[13] Roger Pringle, 'Introduction', *Programme* for *The Manager*, performed by Jasper Britton, Alexandra Gilbreath, Henry Goodman and Richard Burns, at the Shakespeare Centre, 50th Stratford-upon-Avon Poetry Festival, August 24, 2003.
[14] Patrick Query, 'Form and Redemption in *The Manager*', forthcoming in *The Salt Companion to Richard Berengarten*, ed. Norman Jope and Paul Scott Derrick, Salt Publishing, Cambridge, 2011.

positioning along border zones, no other major English poem of our age could have had such a tortuous path towards reception by readers in its own language, while at the same time achieving such consistency of commentary and evaluation from those who have been fortunate enough to discover and respond to it. To conclude this sketch, the scale of its originality and the clarity of its insights are fully recognised by the major theorist of the nuances of modernity, Zygmunt Bauman:

> Many have tried, and many more will try, to crack the mystery of our condition, which is unlike any other we or our fathers or mothers have ever known before. Most have failed: our experience seems to escape any nets sewn of words which have been forced into stiff definitions. But images often say more and, unlike arguments, may be used as mirrors to hold up to the countenance of our experience. Richard Burns is master-supreme of images. His images speak, and they speak of truth that cannot be grasped in any other way.[15]

The publication of this edition of *The Manager* as a single volume in the ongoing series of Richard Berengarten's *Selected Writings* not only initiates the proper and timely contextualisation of this long poem within his own overall oeuvre, but consolidates its position as a major text of European postmodernism. For this edition, appropriately, the author repossesses his ancestral name.

CHRIS HAMILTON-EMERY
JULY 2008

---

[15] Zygmunt Bauman, complete text for back cover commendation, 1st edition of *The Manager: a poem*, 2001. Text supplied by RB.

Acknowledgements

Parts of this book have been published in: *Against Perfection*, King of Hearts, Norwich; *At The Window, for four-part Choir*, Fand Music Press, Petersfield; *Another Chicago Magazine*, Chicago; *Another First Poetry Book*, Oxford University Press; *Boundary 2*, SUNY, Binghamton; *Cheapo Review*, Maidstone; *Equivalencías*, Madrid; *Focus on Literacy*, Harper Collins, London; *For David Gascoyne, on his sixty fifth birthday*, Enitharmon Press, London; *Menadžer*, Writers' Association of Montenegro, tr. Jasna B. Mišić & V. Sekulić; *Mencards*, Menard Press, London; *Mill Road Cam*, Cambridge; *Ninth Decade*, London; *Notre Dame Review*, Uni-versity of Notre Dame, Indiana; *Pembroke Poets*, Pembroke College, Cambridge; *P.E.N. New Poetry II*, Quartet Books, London & New York; *Poetry South East*, Tunbridge Wells; *Roots/Routes*, Cleveland State University Poetry Center, Ohio; and *The Jewish Chronicle*, London. I am grateful to all those responsible for these publications, and above all to my editors and translators in former Yugoslavia, who published the first book-length edition of this work in Serbo-Croat translation, ten years before it appeared in English: *Menadžer*, tr. Jasna B. Mišić & V. Sekulić, Udruženje književnika Crne Gore [Writers' Association of Montenegro], 1990.

Of the many friends who have helped me, I should especially like to mention Peter Mansfield (1942–2008), who was ever-available with patient help and advice, and painstakingly shaped and edited the text; Anthony Rudolf, who has been constant in support and encouragement; and Nasos Vayenas, through whose presence composition ended and began.

RB
CAMBRIDGE
2000 & 2008

The Manager
a poem

Under the plane tree an old woman knits. She has passed beyond need or mourning. She neither frowns nor smiles.

She is patterning our destiny. She is fashioning our future. She is reworking fate. She is making history.

We shall bear her across the river. We shall wear every garment she threads. Each evening we shall wash them

And by night hang them out. They will dry under the stars. Swathed in her images, we'll lie naked until morning.

Part One

One

GEMINI

May 22–June 21

This entire week you need to stay on guard. Rely on old friends only. Be thoroughly critical

Of business speculations. New clients may want something you would be sorry to part with.

Beware of approaches of a romantic nature. Your open, generous character may be undermined.

Developments at work will directly affect your love life. Aim to manage your affairs with tact

And circumspection. Avoid making pledges, promises or vows. Lest untamed angels in disguise

Try to enter your confidence, their forked tails and folded wings hidden beneath their smiles,

Particularly Friday. Admit them on no account. They aim to erode you: wear your words away,

Strip them of meanings, empty your acts of hope, sear and scar your heart, ground the flight

Of your dreams, smother you in sorrow. Over the Bank Holiday you may rot and shrink in their shadow.

And sudden breakdown or memory lapse tumble and flood you in darkness.

Two

Our evenings together, my love, are an economic miracle. Glimpsed
through a one-way window that never opens.

The Man of Sundays looks in. The Man of Timelessness out. Tattoos
are cut in his cheeks and his loincloth

Is pure crocodile. No matter if state subsidised for our educational
benefit, he's nearly large as life

And sandwiched safe between Songs of Praise (which this week
comes to us beamed down from the parish of Bishop's Cleaving

With a final five-minute appeal for the Distressed Mortgage Holders' Fund, a national cause all too close to our hearts)

And our favourite Late-Night Classic, The Sabbatarian Spinechiller,
timed to prime us with suitably resonant nightmares

For the onset of our workweek. Edified by such rich appetisers to
keep us in trim, Africa O Africa, for our regular

Emotional feastings monitored by digital watch, who needs Freud,
needs Guilt. To strains of Oh-Isn't-He-A-Bit-Like-You-And-Me,

Trapped by us in our living room, our crocodile-man can't see anything. He gapes at The World About Us. Never mind.

Tonight it was pork chops. Your eyes are blurred too. At least you've
done snipping out your offers from the colour supplements

And in a little while we both will tumble into breathlessness. One
after the other. In whichever order we come.

Three

Dad I can't get to sleep. I keep sort of hearing creakings. I'm not really afraid but I am

A bit afraid. I think the noises are coming from over there in the corner. Now my little one. Listen.

On top of that shelf the elves are building a castle. In the corner by the desk

A colony of fairies. All made of light and shadow with bodies that shine like angels. No they don't have wings

Like butterflies. They fly with arms like ours. And on the wardrobe a dragon, four inches long.

His scales drink in sunlight. They swivel to catch the rays. So he can fuel the flame he has for a heart.

His nest is a mess because he kills moths and spiders. He chases them out of dream and turns them yes into stars.

And in the fireplace dwarves are digging to the cellar. To mine the glitter from coal and forge bows and arrows and swords

Tinier and finer than needles. That glint on the air like dust. Each one studded with a thousand sparkling jewels.

Four

Well Charles what'll it be. You must be bloody joking. Put a squirt of vodka in it. Hair of the dog. Hail Mary.

How's your patch doing then. Which branch did you say you're handling. Turnover how much. That can't be bad.

Good ole Middlesex. Firm's longest established cock-up. Everything in triplicate but contracts not a dickybird. Cross between

A morgue and the Natural History Museum. So can't say I'm sorry to hear you've been moved up. Fresh blood just what's wanted

And so much the better if you're making a bit of a go at it. Which must take some doing with Wilkins running the Stanmore show.

I suppose he's still there. Or has he been moved down to Staines. Just as I thought. He's been around for donkeys. Part of the F & F.

I say. I don't like the sound of that Charles. Try one of these antacids. New stuff. Swiss or German. Take two each night

Regularly mind. Works wonders you know. What're you eating. Ploughman's right you are. A scampi for me please my love.

No Wilkie's not a bad stick. Loyal as the corgis. But he's nothing but a glorified super-squaddie really. Always on time with his orders

And always sticks by the book. Never should've got past corporal if you see what I mean. All right sergeant I suppose if you must.

Thinks he can handle policy but won't ever go it alone. Keeps shooting off memos and phoning through to the top. I hear Sir K's

Had a bellyful. Poor ole codger should have got his handshake years ago. We'll have to find a way to kick him upstairs. Cheers.

Five

Day invades the curtains. Their ranks are in disarray. A damp breeze

Sends them fluttering and wheeling. Like birds before migration.

In the yellow room next door the children are playing soldiers. You too wide awake

Smoking. The bedclothes rustle around us like a heap of dry leaves.

Six

Dancing half canned at Miriana's party, I mumbled: What do you want? Meaning, From Life. From The World. You laced hands around my neck pressed breasts and belly against me

Hooked eyebeams into mine and coolly said: You. And turned and walked through the dancers. And stood by the front gate, waiting, under white overhanging lilac. A perfumed sprig in each hand.

What's your name? I asked. And, in your raftered attic, with its orange curtains, candles, homepainted mandalas, and tiger balm and saffron scent soaked in cushions and hangings,

Lothlorien Ishtar, you said. I made it up out of books. I change my life every day. So am free to change my name. How old are you? I said. With pointed forefinger you lifted my chin, stepped

Back, unwound your sari, and stood before me naked. This is my real name, you said. This is who I am. And lifting arms sideways: And this, exactly how old. And I, a sudden schoolboy,

Hovered hands around you, as if you were blossoming hawthorn and they a pair of blackbirds, wary of unseen danger, uncertain which branch to settle. Till you pulled me down to your breasts,

Tumbled us onto your mattress, hoisted thighs around my waist and, tearing at my shoulders, cried at the roofbeams. And afterwards, you said, as if reciting a litany: Baba teaches that every cell

Has its inner memory. And flowers of the mind need body's soil to root in. And the light lived by the soul is a body without shadows that outshines all minds. You see. How simple it is.

Yes, I lied. I see. As if lying, half waterlogged, among salt waves summoned by you. Drowning, an unbeliever, among your beautiful clichés. Almost at peace, completed. Almost even believing.

Seven

I yet myself continually. I and myself. I why myself. I think my thoughts are bees. My hopes are silk and money.

My pockets overflow. My head is a promised land I glimpse through mountain haze. My eyes get golden days

But night is elephantine. In my dream a drop of water dies and turns to a round pebble.

Eight

How I piss myself off. Being so polite to them. The Directors and Deputy-Directors. The Customers Clients End-Users. The Strategists Tacticians Negotiators. The Specialists and Expert Consultants. The Marketers and Marketeers. The Banker-Member-Racketeers. The Arbitrators and Advisers and Researchers and Developers.

The Receptionists PAs Telephonists. The Clerics and the Clerks. The Commissioners and Commissionaires. The Porters and the Waiters and those who will not wait. The Internal and External Inspectors. The Plaintiffs and Complainers and Nobodies and Nerds. The Chairmen and their Charwomen – Chairpersons – Charpersons –

The Shareholders and Stakeholders and Contractors and Constructors. The Passionately Believing Reformers and Perfectionist Laissez Faire Dinosaurs. And the Graduates in Bloody Everything these days from Plumbing to Leisure Promotion. The Insurers Assurers Assessors. The Admen and the Admin-Men. Who with almost no exception see themselves as

Models of Efficiency Epitomes of Excellence Examplars of Moral Virtue Upholders of Tradition Prosecutors of Injustice Scourges of Corruption Defenders of Reason and Rectitude Preservers of Rights and Privileges Paragons of Normality stroke Normalcy Patent-Holders of Honor slash Honour. Authorities on Bloody Everything –

Except that all these Paladins of Global Bullshit have to keep haring around faster faster faster in order not to collapse not sink not drown on the spot. As if the whole world were a quagmire they were shit-scared of getting muddied in. Or swamp where a point-zero-zero-three recurring risk of exposure guaranteed deadly infection. All carrying on non-stop

As if the top halves of their heads were permanently sliced off. All behaving as if Pure Dosh were the Total Be-All-and-End-All. Like Hey You Guys I Mean. We All Have The Right. To Survive. Make Ends Meet. Earn An Honest Buck Yen Mark Even Quid. Sheer Necessity Isn't It. So One Does Need to Make Allowances. And of course Perks. But why are they – or we –

All such arseholes?

Nine

CONFIDENTIAL MEMO

To: Ms McPherson   From: Chairman of the Board

1. Owing to opening of new accounts have decided corporation efficiency & prestige wd be considerably enhanced by appointment of personable female in moderately senior admin role operating as

2. Hostess/Consort for international clients. Official duties to include travel/reception arrangements at Heathrow/London City/Gatwick also hotel & theatre bookings cultural/industrial visits etc. Also to provide

3. Individualised secretarial service throughout client's GB stay accompany evenings as & when necessary offer attentive personal support entertainment/hospitality etc. I have in mind

4. Well-spoken well-groomed single or divorced woman aged 24-30 sec/pa training min three A levels inc two B passes one or more languages an advantage. Graduates not to be ruled out but

5. But taste/reliability more relevant. Essential no children or ties. Prefer ambitious practical & wholly dedicated female experienced advertising / marketing / poss tourism who must appear

6. Open friendly be prepared cater new Asian esp Pacific Rim clients etc. Initial salary £14.5K normal contract benefits plus car expenses & flat. Suggest flat in W. Ken / Fulham Rd. area to be

7. Supplied by Prospect & furnished in consultation with appointee who must answer directly to me for all duties maintain strictest confidence & otherwise work independently. Emphasise this as

8. Challenging role in expanding Multinational Company & unique new Prospect service etc. NB appointee must have good London knowledge & of other European capitals. Aim: to promote

9. Overseas potential & turnover. Job-title: International Liaison Officer. Kindly draft contract, commission flat & priority appropriate ad to me listing suitable placements. Shortlist six max.

10. I shall need to see photos.

KWL/GS/30-11

Ten

In tele-sales she said, She was Libra with Leo ascending. Her astrological twin, Janice

She'd met six years ago. Both wheeling prams. Shopping along The Broadway. Janice was born

On the same day exactly. Same year same town and same maternity clinic. Within the hour.

And she and Janice both had three girls. Eleven, nine and seven now. And the names of each

Age-pair began with the same letter. Fran and Fiona. Alison and Annie. Nadia and Natasha.

And then they found they were both married to Edwards. She could quite fancy Janice's Edward

In a non-sexual sort of way. But her Edward didn't fancy Janice. No not at all. Thank Goodness.

So every year since then they'd gone caravanning together. The Broads The Lakes The Peaks

And twice down to Cornwall. The kids of course got on like nobody's business. And their Edwards

Had gone and joined the same sea-angling club. And were thinking now of going into partnership.

And as for the houses, they had just the same pattern curtains and wall-paper in the sitting room

And same matching bathroom suite. It just stood to reason, didn't it, all those things in common

Had to be more than coincidence. When it came to anything important she didn't mind admitting

She wouldn't dream of confiding in anybody but Janice. Janice called the whole thing pure synchronicity.

Eleven

It has never been like this before not with anyone else before, she said. Not with Nick the Prick

Or Roy the Boy or Pete the Meat or even Butch the Navy. God but he was rough with me, that one, she said.

Once he took me back to his place pulling me along the pavement till he nearly yanked my arm off. His shirt tails

Were hanging down below the back of his jacket. God how I loved him then, she said. And another time I remember

We went to some disco in Brighton. Early May and warm and we'd been on the beach all day.

Not warm enough to swim really but he made me take a quick dip, the bastard. And he wore

Rugby shorts to an inch below his knees, with his ordinary socks and black regulation shoes

And that's how we went to the disco. All those kids staring as if we were out of our heads. And we asked for a Golden Oldie

From about, i.e. ten years ago. Six months was ancient history to the little Teenies in there. God I adored him

For that, she said. But It has never been like this not with anyone else before.

Twelve

PROSPECTUS

Come to Topsett. Self-Ownership With A Difference. Where a real sense of community is based on respect for privacy. Residences uniquely and individually styled. Desirably secluded in newly converted parkland. Adjacent to superior modern shopping mall and enviably

Located within convenient reach of City Centre by car or public transport with schools nursery and health care services in nearby vicinity. Designed by an award-winning team of local architects and landscaped to specifications of leading borough-planners

Our imaginatively diversified accommodation comprises both pastoral and metropolitan benefits and is guaranteed to meet the widest variety of specialist and day-to-day requirements ranging from super pied-à-terre penthouses, studios and condominiums for enterprising singles

To 4- and 5-bedroomed homes both detached and semi with spaciously enclosed private gardens front and rear. Personal lockup garages available as extra options on all properties. Residents' Association covers salaried Warden-Caretaker with Assistant on round-the-clock duty

Both Securicad trained and equipped in Warden's Lodge with CCTV burglarproof monitoring system including wall-to-wall emergency searchbeams wired to your own internal alarm panel and your own set of personalised remote-controlled

Gate-keys with buzzer code. Additionally standard precautionary safeguards such as broken glass spikes on walls a plentiful supply of unambiguously worded notices in prominent positions throughout estate to discourage potential intruders such as Private

Topsett Prosp / PTO

Keep Out No Entry No Parking Reserved For Residents Only Trespassers Will Be Prosecuted Guard Dogs Patrol These Grounds. Apply to Topsett Estates Prospect House Gerrards Cross Bucks Tel 01753-007777 Fax 01753-007788 Email topsett@doge.co.uk

With bona fide references. Our specialist finance department is also pleased to offer experienced professional service in arranging your mortgage credit and insurance requirements including life cover on the speediest most advantageous and economic terms.

Thirteen

Hello, she sighs, highly diphthonged. Lovey. Is that you. Guess what my little honeypot. It's sodding

October again and I simply have to celebrate. And guess what else my sugarplum. I need Good Ole You

To help me O. Stave off dem wintry glooms. Steer all dem ghosts away. Rid me of angels tra la. Yeah Make Me Feel So Young.

Well last night I just so happened to find this Poor Pork Joint. An Absolute Whopper. Lying all forlorn and forgotten

In the bottom drawer of my freezer. So I yanks the fellow out. Now he's sitting on my dresser dripping. Simply sweating blood

My duck to be shoved in the oven then wolfed. I'm about to marinade him and stick bits and pieces in him. No need to get

Vulgar sweetipie. I mean garlic and cloves you know I do. But I can't just sit down here and devour the whole thing

On my tod. So why don't you get some togs on and toddle on over. Can you. Really. How super. 'Bout eight then. Bye-hye.

Fourteen

October then. Hunting season. A hot wind from Africa ruffles my thinning hair. No autumn chill tonight on the crisp and sweet night air. I zoom across town with the MG roof down. My cassette blares

From its deck and the folks all stop and stare. Cool who's singing man. Donna Day. Or is it Lady Summer. The Stars Are Out Strolling. The World Is Mine Tonight. With my litre of cutprice Liebfraumilch

Prechilled on the seat beside me. Thus I glide inside the stately gates of Topsett. Destination Pamela. Maisonette 74. Gas Central Heating Double Glazing and Own Private Veranda. Veran-*dah*. I brake

Smartish over two sets of sleepers. Halt beneath sign RESERVED FOR RESIDENTS ONLY. Apples rust quietly on their trees all around. Many alas lie fallen. Scattered over the ground. No gardener

Gathers them. And indeed why should I care. For Pamela is prepared. Or preparing. To indulge with me in an affair. In an *affaire*. Try to forgive me and Lord please pardon her. Before This Night Is Over

May her indulgence be tested. This I dare declare. My prime autumnal prayer. Before her mirror may she now be putting last touches. To all her hairs and hair. Though before I knock *ce soir* I am prepared to swear

She'll have popped in the superette for French Golden Delicious at 78p per lb, sorry £1.30 the kilo. And an economy can of apple purée to drip over her pork. I confess no long-term interest in Pamela's estate. Or in trees

Within these precincts of Topsett. But she as leaseholder sure must have some care or share. Absurd how her fruit rots. How her orchard wastes. How the waste remains and kills. Hello Darling Terrif

To See You I'm perfectly Tickety Boo You Must Be Absolutely Chinkers How Ghastly Poor Duck You're Frozen Just Guess What Happened In Town Today Here Have An Apple. Munch Munch. Roll on *printemps*.

Fifteen

It was love perfect passion abandonment possession. It was complete self-surrender to essence of obsession.

It was heartfelt heavy heaving and knocking on heaven's door. It was fervour and ardour than we'd ever been before.

Sixteen

Boarded the Twin Com and the look on her face said Heaven. Strapped her up front next to me and gave her a pair of phones. Everything A OK. We're cleared to taxi OK.

Wind at ground level 15 knots. Around zero three zero and gusting a bit. Visibility OK. Three knots at three and a half thou. But I go through the checks and would you bloody believe it

There's a drop of over 200 on the port mag. Completely out of parameters and I'm not taking chances with her aboard. So back we go to the shed and Jim says

There's this Beech free. A single. Not quite so swish but OK for a shortish spin. Belongs to Charlie Bollinger. So various hassles later he agrees to hire it out. Finally we're up. Heading for the coast.

VFR and once we're past the Needles it's Cavoc all the way. Look there's our shadow on the foam-flecked waves. Like a day in early June and I ease her into auto. At Ortac 50° North we join

The Mile High Club. And I don't go back on manual till we're past the Guernsey Beacon. Bit of a tight squeeze though. Then this Frog comes on from Brest lousing up the chat.

Allo Golf Alpha Yankee Whisky Sierra. Squish please. You are free degrees off course. Shadow oh my shadow. No no ice thanks just a dash of water OK. Do you read me. Over.

Seventeen

As a child on the playground edge you'd already heard death babbling in *Ring a Ring o' Roses* and *When Sally was a Baby*, as you stopped breathless in your tracks to watch the ceaseless droll parade

Of Bulldog Leapfrog Hopscotch Tag, and the whirling spinning clapping in the centre of the arena, where the girls marked out their circles and the boys rang rings around them, hands locking, interlacing,

With their claspings and their freeings, and their comings and their goings, their tiptoeings, to-and-fro'ings, their scorings and their tracings, their grimacings and their facings and their roarings and their racings

And the gaspings and the cheerings and the trickings and deceivings and the jeerings and the fearings, and the piercing dreams and hushes and the graspings and unmaskings and the rushes and the screams, and the total

Forgivenesses of errors and reliefs from nightmare terrors. And although you'd understood then you could Not Escape The Pattern – you'd heard its sap swell up inside you – even then you'd paused to wonder

What would it be like, to be dead. To be not here, or anywhere. Simply not to be here. How inconceivable. How totally terrifying. How very weird and strange. And even then you'd thought, *How consoling, to be*

Nothing. To drift off, like snow. Into the snow-kingdom. Away, into sleep. Or just to melt, to un-be. When a voice inside you welled, from some stiller, deeper space: *But not ever to have been born? And never*

To have seen this? Not to have stood on this ground or breathed this airy air? Well It's Oh Sir No Sir No Sir No. This will not do for me. I want. I want to. I mustn't. I won't. I was not made for death. I just *refuse* to die.

Eighteen

Coming in Wintersfield. Coming in now. Their front row's gone and collapsed again. Come on Collingswood. Get your heads down. Shove. Two minutes to go. You can do it with a bit more effort. Show us what you're made of. Heel the thing Maurice. Cleanly back and break.

That Prosser Minor's coming on splendidly. Beautiful pass Harmsworth. Well Handled Boy Well Done. And that Lawdon youngster is going to go a long way. See that dodge and side-step. That change of direction and spurt. That's what I call teamwork. Don't boot it into touch

Get it back to Wencott. You super boy what a wristflick. Now out along the line. Yes all the way out. Fifteen seventeen. This must be our last chance to score. That Bruno on the wing can fly like an archangel. Now for God's sake don't waste it. Go Go Go Boy. Go.

What in hell is he doing. He's standing gawping stock still with it. Two yards from their line. Not a soul within miles of him. He's turning round he's laughing he's twirling it in his hands. I just don't believe it. He's gone and knocked it on. Deliberately I'd say.

That little idiot has thrown the game away. The rotten little runt. I don't call that sportsmanship. He deserves to be carpeted. Scratched from the team. Sacked from the school. A disgrace is what I'd call it. He's let the whole side down. He's ruined the whole season.

Nineteen

As she stripped she seemed to take off everything. Including death and memory. Her bangles bracelets rings she dropped in a heap on the dresser. Her panties she discarded with a swift sharp-angled kick. Just as a winged ephemerid on the point of its first flight

Cracks its redundant shard and slithers onto air, with unrehearsed movement, yet as though in measured dance, she seemed to break in pieces the seamless husk of now, drill time's clustered surfaces, cut through faults in its strata. Nakedness within nakedness.

All she kept on was her smile, until in haze, it haloed her, then swallowed us both, weightlessly. Her embrace, firm and yielding, was total as the touch of water. And as we climbed and dived, into and through each other, like two liquids in solution –

Or like twin moons, alternating – or unruffled snowy mountains, mirrored in each other's lakes: I fell, or soared, unforgetting, into precognition, into a storyless zone, before birth or conception. And waking, or sleeping, cried – or was it she who cried? –

What is it we have done, that what we were or would be weighs so heavy on what is, and what we might become yields only what has been through us, as though we had recognised nobody, least of all ourselves, other than as most inconsequential strangers?

And she, or another voice, replied, through whom, half drowning, I woke: Although this self-loss might hint another order, a wakefulness we flow towards, for us there is but the one river. Now, only sleep and rest. There will be time enough later for time.

Twenty

Am I stealing you from your husband or leasing you from God. We move so very high together, even among platitudes.

The fields the rivers the forests the unassailed peaks. And all the tarnished metaphors

Are somnolent in your smile. They shimmer there, made radiant. Ah yes, the latitude of platitudes.

The glens and the dales. The vales and the veils. And the silence between them. This light that nothing fails.

Tell me how have you been. And how are your children. Have you missed me. I've missed you. You haven't. I have, you know.

Yes I do know yes. Your touch is white light and you smile upon me the rainbow. Your naked body clothes

Your naked body in glory. Oh turn over, please. Just turn over softly. Come close to me.

Twenty-One

Some people you can tell by no more than a single glance at them

Aren't going to live very long. And you love them all the more for it. Sometimes

I think you're like that. But I want you to live a thousand years.

Twenty-Two

One Thursday I skipped school and took myself to a matinée. I was in the lower sixth and a virginal sixteen year old. Full of hopes. Of dreams. I wore my Sunday suit. The play was something by Ibsen. I paid my two and six

And sat high in the Gods in the almost empty theatre. And in the second interval wandered down to the buffet to buy an orangeade. The bar-hall, long and deserted. Only one person, sipping a drink at the counter. A thickset woman,

Big breasted. Full-lipped. Who stared, as if through me. Beckoned. I, well brought up to obey any adult's call, took self-conscious steps towards her. Her bulbous eyes seemed magnets, protruding from her head.

Hairs on my arms stood. I was about to say, Did you want . . . ? when she, in broken voice, You're Charles I know, aren't you. I could swear for a split second I saw your father Philip. I thought I'd seen a ghost. And she began to weep.

Oh Uncle Phil. Such a fine man. He dandled me on his knee. How are the mighty fallen. Tears streamed down her cheeks, runnelling rouge and mascara. She collected herself. How do you do, Charles. I am your cousin Una.

Maybe you have heard of me. I am here only a day. I used to come and play with you when you were a baby. I knew you by your eyes your walk your face your hair. Tell me, my fine young man. Are you happy in your life?

I, Prince of Hesitation, terrified she would touch me, gauchely stuttered extracts from my stock of teenage platitudes. The third act bell rescued me. We shall meet again, she said. I turned in quiet terror, sensing her eyes on my back. Though I move still in darkness, I know she, or her like, already waits for me at the other end of my story. And much and deep have I dwelt in my heart on her promise of recognition.

Twenty-Three

He's a lurcher not a whippet, said Steve, shifting his bulk from his bar stool to pat the creature's head. Nice colouring, eh. It's that white patch over the eye gives him that wistful harlequin look.

He can sniff out a pheasant at 300 yards. Go for it like Casanova. A little on the big side but he sleeps under the duvet. Don't you old feller. Two more Harvests and another Dubonnet please, Ray.

Watcher mean Casanova, sniffed Vicky petitely between us, nudging him in the ribs. At least he doesn't snore. Which is more than can be said for some people. Your pullover smells like a museum,

She said, and turned on me, conspiratorial. You ever seen him without it. He won't let me wash it. Never takes it off. Sleeps in it too, you know. Says it's got Special Sentimental Value. Cobblers.

And what with him and Hound Dog here hogging the bed between them, it's a bleeding miracle I get any sleep at all. And in the morning, she said, snuggling her neck into his giant elbow

And addressing the bar at large, His breath's like a filthy ashtray. What I have to put up with, she sighed, I don't know why I bother. You're not exactly Nice, you know. Not what I'd call Respectable.

I don't know about that, I said. He looks all right to me. No nasty infectious diseases. And he doesn't squint or stammer. What more do you want. He can't help being small. What about a game of darts.

Rather watch the pro's, said Steve. 'S an international on. He ferried our drinks to the public bar and sat at an empty table. The dog wagged its tail and snoozed on its ribcage and haunches.

The TV blared in the corner. Darts is made of tungsten, confided the commentator. And you need tungsten nerves for this game. This lad's a son of Peterborough. If he wins this final or not

They're giving him a civic reception when he gets home tomorrow. If he was my son I tell you I'd give him Peterborough. I hear they show Shakespeare on BBC 2. But you can't beat darts for drama.

His table manners aren't bad, said Vicki. And, true, he hasn't got rabies. He's just a great big healthy animal. Aren't you eh, Midget. What about foot and mouth, said Steve. Disgusting man, she said.

Twenty-Four

You are a true blue brick Tony and she knows which side her bread's buttered on. She has the good salt taste

Of mortar in her mouth. As she dreams of your large lawn and studies double-glazing. Well indeed you both manage

Mortgage estate and marriage. Your joint account in Prospect National also comes in handy. As does your Maplan Policy.

Providing her shelf of *huiles* and *crèmes* in recently pink tiled bathroom. With perfect patterned matching suite

Of shower bidet and vanity cabinet. Where age lifts mirrored faces to smile between manicured hands.

And also your blue BMW you willingly let her drive. Whose wheel she handles noiselessly however small she feels in it

Never scraping the gears. And what with your two super children, both doing well at St. Hilda's,

And although she will have her weeps, and a whinge or two now and then, and although she only comes, so she says,

When she lies down with me, and although we don't discuss that now and I'd never spoil auld lang syne

By bothering you with this, old fellow (after all, what's friendship if it's not keeping your mouth shut)

No she will never leave you. One hundred percent reliable. You've invested well there boy.

Twenty-Five

Your silence squeezes me dry. If I were you my finish would be different. A sparrow shits on the fence. I see him

Through the pane your curtains don't quite cover. Still my left hand cups your left breast.

Dawn turns up its volume. Faint signals grow in my legs. They begin to speak in audible English voices. I think I had better

Go home now. To my wife. You are about to say something in a language I don't understand. I slide into my clothes. They fit.

Your turn your back to me and your arms clutch the pillow. Through the long mirror your eyes scrape my skin.

A siren goes off in my head. I take it off the hook. I give my number. Coming, I say. Coming.

I wade through your gaze to the door.

Twenty-Six

Am I interrupting you? Are you in the middle of things? she enquired, as she poked her head round the door. Oh Sugar, I said,

You've broken my concentration, I can't keep up with anything I'm supposed to be getting on with. I just don't know how I'll manage.

Who supposes? She said. Is it *them* or *you*? *Them*, I said. It's a deadline. Got to be finished Thursday. I just don't know how I'll cope.

And brushed one hand through my hair. And threw both arms back, dramatic. Oh po-oor you, she said. How suffereth the working man.

Well it's *me* I suppose, I ventured. I want to get it done right. Not let anyone down. *And* show the bastards I'm up to it.

In my own thick ears the reasoning sounded flat and flatulent. But I let the statement hang. Waiting for its effect.

Course you do, she said. But who'll give a tinker's if just for once you don't? You Expect Too Much Of Yourself. Really You Do Darling.

She advanced and stood behind me, placed gentle hands upon me, and kneaded my shoulder muscles. I flinched, but didn't turn.

Sorr-ee, she said, rising. It's about time you realised there's a difference between Action and Activity. You don't know which is which, do you.

And all this stress isn't good for you. You ought to take a breather. You're turning trivialities into your proper little EL EE PEE.

Here we go again, I yawned. What's that supposed to mean? Another of your latest buzz-words? Some fancy new-fangled acronym?

Life Evasion Program, she said. The Puritan Ethic's one thing. But you don't have to kill yourself working just to prove you're alive.

Have it your own way, I said. And turned back to the screen, ignoring her. Trying without success to gather lost insignificant thoughts.

Be Reasonable, she said. Why Can't You Be Normal For Once? I don't see why we can't spend a decent evening together. Buzz Buzz, I sneered.

Everybody who's born, she heaved. Into this stupid world. Has an equal right to be in it. You Stupid Stupid Bastard. I'm going out. Without you.

Twenty-Seven

She had a curious way of saying Yes and No together. Once I remember when her husband was away

We lay on her living room carpet by the convector heater. And massaged each other for over an hour without exchanging a word.

Then she lay on her back, naked. And said, I want your child. She liked being squeezed. Much of our time we spent weeping together.

Her English was fluent but she never got rid of her accent. I shall not meet her again off the train or at the airport.

Can you hear me? Are you there? There's somebody else on the line.

It is the dead. Who will not lie down and rest.

Twenty-Eight

You're pretending again, she said. What you really are is a Bastard. Your whole life's One Big Act

And you act as if you're not pretending. Or maybe you really believe it, she said. I always thought you were stupid

But you just can't be that stupid. Or maybe you can, She said. Maybe you're so stupid you think you're being extra clever

Wrapping up your cleverness in stupidity. Like a parcel in dirty paper. I don't know which is worse, she said.

Knowing you're pretending and pretending you don't know. Or believing you're not really pretending really. Unless

You believe you're pretending to be a Bastard. And really think you're not one underneath the act. I did suspect

You were quite bright really, she said. In a stupid sort of way. But you couldn't be that bright. Could you. Eh, stupid.

Twenty-Nine

What's a woman like me to do, she said. This whole town's choc-a-bloc with fragile graduate wimps

Sporting overblown egos. Thin lips, wispy beards. Latest trends in Ecosquirm. Pin-striped Mon-Fri. Weekend shell suits smelling like jumble sales

And no-go areas of wounded sensibilities. Sure they can wax eloquent about Virtual Reality. Real Life Role-Play. Networking in Cybersmog

And Hacking or Downloading off the Intergalactic Super-Web. And sure, pints and pints of randy bijou plumbers. All dinky twenty-five year-olds, she said.

But who wants that for Godsake as a Lifetime Proposition. What is there to talk about with the poor bloke afterwards. And then there are the ones

Who've simply gone off like cheeses. Exhausted their shelf-life. Passed their sell-by date. Nice to talk to, to look at. But dry or mouldy inside.

And the one thing they all have in common, she said, is: Stick them in front of a Real Woman and they wouldn't know which end was which.

Do you know, she said, I met a delightful Slav. Well an utter bastard really. In Yokohama at a conference. *Draga*, he intoned. What You Need Is A Man.

I mean Someone Like Me. Someone to Look After You. Someone to Respect Your Work. Someone to Honour and Care for You. And not let you out of his sight.

Then I explained. There are no such likely lads in the length and breadth of England. He just couldn't understand. Why should he? But anyway, she sighed,

I need that like I need a hole in the head. He didn't add my part of the bargain of course. Sockwashing and cooking his goulash. As for the divorcees

They're all half-pickled or simply haven't grown up. Never got over their prefects and aren't likely to do so in bed. I tell you Darling at my age

There's simply something slightly kooky about any man not accounted for. With the single exception of you, of course. Only trouble is, You, my duck

Fit my professional life-plan just about as perfectly as if I were to turn up at Ascot flaunting an Army & Navy greatcoat. Oh sod it all, she grinned,

And tossed down a throatful of my best Australian Sauvignon. From a glass that had come to me free with MAPLAN lead-free petrol coupons.

Thirty

My name? *Homo aspirans*. Incipient man. With warts on my hands. As I drive in and out of this city. And from one city to another. Across dangerous deserts between fixed appointments. Wildernesses between known addresses. Mined No Man's Lands between filling stations.

If I go on at this rate I'm going to bust a gut. *Congestion on M4*, gloats the contralto announcer on Jazz FM Travel Update. *An overturned container. Oil spillage. Four mile tailbacks between Junctions 10 and 11. Traffic flow eastbound reduced to one crawling lane. So do please*

Take an alternative route if you can. Well I can't because there isn't one. How stupid can they get. I know every trick in the book. All the ins and outs in the region. Back lanes and short cuts like the back of this hairy hand. So that's bloody that then. Home late tonight as usual.

This is no damn good. I will just not go on doing this. I will not go on telling my children lies. Or my team of part-time surrogates for love. Deployed on a non-permanent freelance consultancy basis. As and when the need arises. Until further notice. No strings attached.

Lies to clients and customers. Lies to friends colleagues competitors. Lies to boss and bank manager. Lies to accountant and taxman. Lies to peers and protectors. Lies to waiters and well-wishers. Lies to all the ladies. Yes lie down won't you please lie down ladies.

Sure I Can Manage All Right Thank You Indeed Very Much. That's what I'll say if He asks me. Adding: But Incidentally You See Dear Editor Dear Doctor Dear Chairperson Dear God – all I need is a temporary overdraft. Just to tide me over. Yes M'Lud Yes Ma'am I certainly do have

Full confidence in my own cunning and kenning. In my own personal package of performance prowess proficiency. And am prepared to vouch for my responsibility competence and constancy in states of dispassion and alertness. That I can man this proud vessel HMS *Loneliness*

Entirely single-handed is indeed self-evident and has never been in doubt. *Mah Mammy Done Told Me* . . . howls the FM Blues Singer. Moorbridge. Friary Wells. Avalon-on-Avon. Shuckleford. The villages flicker past. I glide onto the motorway. The signal gets louder and clearer as

This cellular bubble, clasped in its cloud of static, this hollowed splinter of metal, this magnetised personal capsule – is tugged big-citywards. And the only hint of crackle under flyovers or pylons . . . *Mah Daddy Said It Right. Son, If You Go On Doin' The Way You Do*

You're Gonna Drop Right Out of Sight . . . No of course no question of more borrowing or remortgaging. Just normal cashflow problems. I'll wear my most confident smile, and, Yes, that's what I'll say. Ho Ho, I'll beat the whole damn system. Scathed I may be. But I have come of age.

Thirty-One

She's watching *The Holocaust* smoking and paring back her cuticles
glued to Episode Six. During the break it's

Wail Meat. A well meant bonus for Pussikins. For owners of fur skins
and foreskins. Oh wettened white maid, well made

For purse-value, for purr-valour: How smoothly runs The New Princi-
pessa. On AMGLO Grade Z Oil. Bulletin, Bully Tin, Bullet In:

Word-salad out of deep freeze with microwave image-broth, set alight
by satellite across the wheeled wild world: The New

American Bible in authoritative translation, with a free statue of God
cradling The Infant Baba in gold-plated plaster

From Bee Cheese: twice as nutritious as honey but half the calories.
Grate it, slice it, toast it. Or melt it, whiter

Than white. See our beaches, our islands. Timeless masterpieces. Wait-
ing. For You. Now. Holiday in Mamaia. Final solution

To all your washing problems. Our apocalyptic message will change
your kitchen forever. For Purity, The Choice

Is Now Uniquely Yours. Take it, today, with MAPLAN. Sign your life-
sentence to Top Security. To strains of

Hack-Up-Your-Doubles-In-An-Old-Bitch-Hag, and Devotional
Hours to Wall Street, Bonn, Bruxelles, Tokyo, Zurich,

Walls taller than Berlin's blockade us, each from each. Lock us out
from speech. Till bed-time when, beseeching

Rattling bodies reach. To Cape Town then I came. O Lord Thou.
Dresden Nagasaki Sarajevo. Burning Burning Burning.

Thirty-Two

This morning every object in this house conspires against me. Where are you, Come here, I shout at my wallet and folio.

My watch has gone into hiding. My keys are in the wrong jacket. My coffee cup slips from shaking hand and smashes on the floor.

Even toothpaste and razor have disappeared from the bathroom shelf. Outside a pale sun bleeps on a crisp October day

Summoning me clearly, Come out you fool, and enjoy me. I tell myself, Stop hurrying. Stop stopping. There is time.

But I have to make a long journey. And the briefcase which contains my most secret and important documents, absolutely vital

To get past the patrols, has joined the resistance movement. Unless the Secret Police have already got their gloves on it

And managed to prise open its combination lock. Yes I can see them, officers in long trenchcoats with grey fur cuffs and collars

Deciphering my codes, grinning at my misdemeanours, chuckling as they prepare their case to send me into exile,

Striding in knee-length jackboots around their poky office, a damp hut near the border, with its beige shiny walls

And smoking charcoal stove that doesn't keep out the cold, while they go on drinking sweet lukewarm tea beneath the Chairman's portrait

And the snow goes on falling outside. And shall I panic, I wonder, when they call for me in the night. For how can I leave this house

Even now, with nothing I own. And when angels knock, unexpected, and a black sun is shining, how can I go with them, naked, into snow.

Thirty-Three

Is that the telephone ringing. Or is it something in me. I feel as though I had just made love with the Goddess.

Opened my heart to her. Known her depths of kindness. In a state of unforgetting. And been found not wanting.

And as you were putting your clothes back on, I said, like a boy: Amazing. You're flesh and blood.

An ordinary woman. And lay back and dozed. Thinking or half thinking: Who cares. You're my Goddess anyway.

Now you've zoomed off to your place to change into warmer clothes. On the way out you poked your head back round my door.

Wouldn't it be fun to be a Goddess Really, you said. I'll be back in twenty minutes. Goddesses don't get cold.

Thirty-Four

Gasparo Napolitano in fullest flight. Hot from San Diego in the Pearl Room at the Ritz. His bosomy accompanist, a West Coast Carmencita, meticulously preserved. Verdi and Stephen Sondheim. Bernstein and Pagliacci. How for God's sake does he carve that funny little beard

Out of his face without nicking his chin, asks my divorcee companion who has just got in from Minorca where she sells homemade batik. His papa was Italian but his Ma pure Connemara. All iz accents err purrfict but tonight he's real pissed off. And No, His Irish Eyes Aren't Smiling.

He has a problem in creating like *contact* with his *audience*. Who have paid their 60 quid for The Full London Experience. And maybe the chat and the nosh. In the very act of singing he rehearses his self-defence. It Was *Barbaric* They Weren't Even *Listening* I've Never Felt So *Insulted*.

At the next table a Dickhead, True-Blue-Public-School-City, British International-Ilk and Exaggeratedly Yah, bangs his fork on the table and grunts *Moah Moah* as he canoodles with his blonde popsie after It's A Long Long Time From May To September just before the lemon sorbet

As though ten seconds before time his team's fly half had saved the match by dropping a stupendous goal. Gerald opposite me, our Swiss Cottage solicitor, so *he* ought to know, leans over, conspiratorial. *He's a top consultant in Cheapside*, he mumbles. *Was at school, you know,*

With Hoggson. Junior Defence Minister. Perfectly above board of course. I firstguess Gerald is referring to our blithe Gasparo. Then I work it out. Gerald means the dickhead. Something to do with arms deals. Britain to Iraq via Austria. Or Iran to Croatia via Hungary. Or Turkey.

Or Bulgaria. What difference does it make. Napolitano controls his timbres and glissandos as firmly as his grimace and ego. And three times more obviously. Like a tube train roaring through a Euston tunnel, his diminuendo reverberates within the inner ear. He oozes insincerity and

A star is in the making. So he sings for twenty minutes instead of the prescribed forty-five. Which is what he's being paid for. Gerald rabbits on. Ins and outs of divorce procedures. Unreliable clients. How to win the lottery. God he's so damn nice. I can't make out which is worse

The audience or the singer. *Nella profondità del mio cuor io appartengo a voi due.* How I bore most myself. For no reason at all I expound the Theory of Duende. Everybody yawns. At the big table in the corner the Japanese group rustles off to taxis. And the leaves dwindle down.

Thirty-Five

So that afternoon she flits with the consultant. Comes back three hours later than we'd arranged at lunch. Says it was awful that she wished she hadn't done it

That neither had enjoyed it and she was damn well going out again. What about the party, quietly I ask her. What party, she demands, nibbling at the ham.

Sam's and Rowena's, I say, Don't you remember. Invited us last week. Oh that, she says. Why not. And flounces off upstairs. To bathe arrange her demi-wave

And select her utmostly slinky. Descends two hours later in a silk greeny sleeveless dress. The whole kitchen drowns in her catch-me scent.

We're late and I drive as usual. Look, I say. Can we agree. Just to enjoy the party. You do your own thing and I'll get along with mine, she says. The usual crowd there. Executives Shrinks

Hacks. I stand in the long kitchen and chat up a lanky blonde. I've written to Up Front, she says, About Bluebell Wood. Everyone ought to go there. It's such a super place.

Then drift into the living room and dance with David's wife. Who's still teaching Geography at the Poly and St. Hilda's. Moderately nice tits but tonight I fancy nothing.

Plonkful I roam the room. Get myself plastered and call some twerp a bastard. He asks, Who is this creep. I Eff him and he backs down. Then look for Sheila.

Who is dancing with Tony. Pissed out of her tiny. Here we go. I know. She stares right through me and snuggles closer to him. I perch on a couch edge suddenly feeling foul. Who's that

Lovely creature with the green dress silky voice, I half hear some contralto richly ooze beside me. That. Is my wife, I hear myself reply. She turns to the leggy blonde to carry on as before.

Aroma Therapy. Feng Shui. Battered Wives. Single Mothers. Male Strippers. The Arjuna Commune. Viagra and HRT. Tony and Sheila slip away upstairs. Slowly I rise,

Find Rowena. Give her the car keys. For Sheila, when she comes down. Rowena nods expressionless. Slight drizzle outside. Night air feels good as I walk down Milton Drive.

Thirty-Six

Yes hello there Looie hello. What can I do for you. Yes I'm on the road and it's really pissing down. Hold on a mo will you while I get into this layby. What's that again. I can't hear a word. Can *you* hear me.

Again please. The Takhirev meeting's postponed. *What* meeting. And till *when*. Till Tuesday next at three. Right let me find my organiser. OK Got it I'll be there. But hang on will you. Who the hell is Takhirev. What did

You say *She*. Looie it can't be a *she*. The women are all *-ova* or *-eva* over there. No not over. I mean oh vee ay. Like eggs mate in Latin. No Looie I *know* it's not an ancient Roman. And no never *Eva* either. But

Their women's names have got tails on. Ha Ha very funny. Looie I mean special endings. God you are so *crass*. OK so you've met her and you do have reason to believe he really is a she. No Looie I don't give

A monkey's toss what kind of armoured vehicle she's built like or whether she's amphibious or how low she floats in the water or how broad in the beam she is or even how uneven the distribution

Of her facial follicles or whether you could fancy her for a hirsute hump in the hay. God It beats me how fucking dyslexics like you could ever have got into this game. No Looie not dyspeptics. Look Looie just

Forget it will you it really doesn't matter No I'm not having you on I'm not taking the piss and Don't give me another dose of your I-went-to-a-comprehensive-in-Scunthorpe stuff. Looie Looie can you please just

Listen to me for Godsake All I'm doing is trying to extract one single marginally accurate byte out of your pea-brain while I'm stuck in some lousy fucking layby on this fucking dual carriageway. Yes Looie I do

Like you I positively adore you You're the pig's pickled trotters No I can't live without you either Yes I know it's wholly mutual Honest. So let's get this straight and start again from scratch can we. Looie Yes I am

Getting this down now Hang on a mo. What's that. Director of Settlements and Clearance Division for *what*. No it's no good it's breaking up again can you repeat that please. *CompostBank*. Looie it

Can't be *Compost* it must be something else. OK I'll see if I can dredge it up. Looie wait wait I've got it Yes I do know what you're on about for once. It's *Kompas*. kay oh em pee ay ess. Damn Can you hear.

Like sextants. Like all sailors have one. Like charting your passage. Like checking your course by the stars. Looie Will You Please Stop Shouting At Me No I Am Not Pissing You Around I Swear. OK Yes now I can

Hear you that's better. I know *exactly* who you're talking about she's the VIP Sir K's been expecting from Something Stan. Tavak or Takav or something. God Bless You Too Comrade Looie. Looie Mate Thank You

Very much.

Thirty-Seven

A lecture on the University of the Third Age's *Linguistics For Everybody* Course. Title: *Purging Obsolescent Notations*. Speaker: Dr. Muriel Thorpe, Reader in Gender and Communication Studies at the newly constituted CPU (Corsington Polytechnic University).

We really must go, darling, says Susan. So we sit in the third row. Oh look, there's Nadine, she says. And waves. You know, from next door but one. But, knitting, Nadine does not notice us. 'The alternatives *he* stroke *she* stroke *it*,' intones Dr. Thorpe, 'constitute an algorithmic tree

Of marked and unmarked gender notations. The taproot, i.e. deep structure, traditionally classified by those of you ahem fortunate or unfortunate enough to remember having done er Classics at school as third person singular nominative pronoun, generates the trunk, i.e.

Unmarked form, *he*, while the marked branch on as it were the right hand side of the string, depending of course which angle you're viewing it from, gives us *she*. And if *she* stroke *he* are (or rather *is*) considered, in turn, higher up as it were or, if you prefer, lower down,

As constituting a single unmarked variant here on the um er left hand side, the formulation *it*, commonly delineated as neuter, is undoubtedly the marked form in this second binary opposition. Now, the new notation-set which *we* propose to deploy henceforward to replace

The rather unwieldy, archaic Latinisms and even ha *Chomskyisms* of masculine-dominated linguistics, and – here, let me write it for you onto this slide so you can all get it off the screen and all just jot it straight down, I'll use this nice green marker I think, – is S/H/IT.'

There is not a single eyeblink. No trace of cough or stutter. Nor a cocking (or cunting) of eyebrows. Only devoted gazes. Just the loyal fluid glide of rollerballs and ultrafine felt-tips. Smoothly sliding across twenty seven lined punched recycled pages. Except for Nadine

By the wall, who carries on knitting and yawning. Well, I think, why shouldn't she. 'Now while this will serve as our theoretical benchmark,' continues Dr. Thorpe at precisely the same speed, 'or at least our pedagogic base, we note that the real *pragmatic* situation is rendered even

More complex by pronouns which substitute *she* for vehicles which in the past tended to be operated more or less exclusively by human personnel of the masculine gender, for example water vessels like *ships, yachts, boats* and the like, and more recently *cars, mopeds, motor bikes* . . .'

Brilliant, says Sue afterwards, Absolutely brilliant. Hi Nadine How Are You. Bye Nadine. Bye. See You Soon. Now let's chill out with a drink. We must come again next week. Mustn't we darling. Cool, I venture, shyly and for the first time ever. I'd like to do that. Cool. Real cool.

Thirty-Eight

Tonight she's in bed with her Cypriot. Her balmy long-legged barman. I know because I phoned. Karolos or Kostas or What's His Name. I can't remember, as usual. Her voice was the same one she uses

When someone's in the same room with her. And she's moderately pissed. All clammy loose and upper crust and highly diphthong-laden. Three vowels to each syllable where normally one would do. Pointedly I said

Am I interrupting, and she went all coy and formal. Not At All Oh Hello It's You. It's Okay There's Only Takis Here. And Anyway, It's Not Important. And I thought, Okay Only Takis. Here-O Fear-O Queer-o.

And remembered Sunday lunchtime when I'd driven her out to The George. And she'd sat at the bar all preeny smiling her smiliest smile. And leaned towards me and murmured through purse-lipped exhalations

With legs twined tight round the bar stool twirling stiletto tips and nipples pointing bra-less through her rayon stretchfit popover, I Say Don't Look Now Darling But Doesn't He Look Rather Nice

That Tall Chap Over There I Mean. I Do Like his Teeth. And through a puff and a giggle: I Simply Adore His Accent. And a couple of gins later (was she trying to tell me then): Do You Know Darling

He Has Such Big Brown Eyes. This bit. Casually inserted. While talking about something else. Made this somehow seem. The most. Important. Thing. Of all. Perhaps precisely. Because of. Its lack of.

Importance. *His Big Brown Eyes.* Ridiculous. And her own eyes at that moment. Impenetrable black wells. What was his name again anyway. Larky Sparky Taki? I can't remember, as usual.

We promised each other the truth but we play it as a game and cheat at it. I wish I didn't know I wish I hadn't phoned. I never want to see you again God God I want you.

Thirty-Nine

Cover me Manoula. Let me die on your granite breast. Lull me to sleep under your grey snow.

The stars hurt my eyes. The black night dazzles. The offshore breeze singes my hair.

Take the rainbow away. Lock it up in a vault. If it comes any closer its pincers will throttle me.

Draw the clouds across. Sink your teeth in my eye sockets. Gently shut the lids with your barnacled fingers.

Sear me with your lava. Root your weeds through my pores. Anchor your dark in my white coral bones.

Forty

Now it's autumn your headaches have migrated south. You know
you haven't had one really

Since 1989. And know I know you know. So now it's a straight
No delivered where it hurts. Sure

I can take it. And whatever else you can't give. Till I get my night
out Friday. And my own back.

I should know. We've been married long enough. Though tonight
surprise surprise there's this

Proud thing here between us. That's funny isn't it. After how long
lain low. But no it is not a weapon. Or hammer

Tool jack-knife rod. It is very part of myself. And could be yours
again too. Oh Go On. Please Love. Just This Once.

Okay Okay. Have it your own way. How true. I don't want you.
All I'm after's a Screw. No thanks I can manage

Perfectly well by myself thanks. No Don't Look. Go back to your
damn book. Just pass me

That magazine from the bottom shelf in the cabinet. O thou who
chariotest to their dark wintry bed

The wingèd seeds. Where they lie cold. And Lola. And Ingrid
Danielle Erika. And centrefold Sylvie.

And Ishtar Astarte Ashtaroth. And Artemis Lilith Eve. And thine
azure sister. Rondinella Rondinella.

Stuff the emotion. Where's the tissue and lotion. Ashes and sparks.
My words among mankind.

Forty-One

Sipping Earl Grey in the Orangerie at the Park Lane Four Seasons, she crosses and recrosses her legs and recounts her latest escapades. Stephanie, she says,

You know my lovely friend Stephanie. Well she's just getting over five children and Dicky just ups and walks out on her. They've a charming little place somewhere

Up near Chipping Camden. And of course she can't afford the repayments poor thing, not all by herself. Might even get repossessed. So while she's kicking her heels and being reshaped and manicured

Waiting for that so-called husband of hers to sort himself out – or at least show up and do something marginally useful – Stephanie zooms down to London to mingle with weekend Sloanes.

Sometimes she stays over at my place. Sometimes with someone else. Then she bumps into Old Thingummy at some do or other. Peter Townley-Warner or Rupert Patchwork-Quilt,

I can't remember which but you know the one I mean. Bête grise and eminence noire alias Ghastly Warthog. Yes frightfully bald these days but still absolutely reeking of pheromones.

Well, he calls her up the other day on his dinky mobile. Probably while stuck in some traffic jam. Says, Darling, Isn't that absolutely charming daughter of yours coming out at last.

I can't afford that, she snaps. I've got enough on my plate with five of them to look after. And I'm not a miracle worker. It's Dicky who's coming out. Next month. Out of

Ford Open. After three years ruminating that multi-million fraud of his. What an absolute scream. Well she's got to get back at him somehow hasn't she. One certainly does get around.

I say. Don't look now darling. But over there by the coconut palm. To the left of the chandelier. There's a small impotent-looking man. And he's wearing my daughter's knickers.

Forty-Two

Far too many years, Oh Great Schmuck of a Boss. Have I lain awake nights till three or four a.m. Brooding in fantastic rehearsal

What I should say to your face at ten o'clock next morning. When I, in the General Office, already seated an hour at my desk,

Observe you just arriving. In tailor-made silk-lined pin-stripes. In debonair Old School Tie. Financial Times tucked pinkly

Under your left arm. In time for your first appointment. In your panelled inner sanctum. With its dimmers and dictaphone.

Its drinks-and-crystal cabinet. Its red leather-padded chairs. Its lion-legged mahogany table. Its panel of digital switches.

Its portraits of previous MDs. Sterling silver cigar box polished on your desk. Envelope-opener topped by Company logo . . .

That you are a Dictatorial Power-Hungry Stingy Selfish Unscrupulous Manipulative Conniving Nefarious Flagitious Amoral Pasty-Faced . . .

But each time it came to it, smiled. And uttered not a word. Other than *Good Morning Sir Keith*, as you zoomed past, unnoticing,

Nor even added *You Bastard* under my breath, *You Slimy Mean Pompous Bloodsucking Twisted Bastard*. Even though I have suffered my own

ABC of Miseries. Acidity Backache Colitis. Anoxia Bronchitis Catarrh. Agnosia Borborygmus Claustrophobia. Dyspepsia

Eczema Flatulence. Diarrhoea Endocarditis Furunculosis. Gastritis Heartburn Insomnia. Gonorrhoea Halitosis Incontinence.

Not to mention Irritable Bowel Syndrome. Repetitive Strain Injury. Sick Building Syndrome. To Zeugmatitis and Zugzwang...

You Tight Arsed Hypocrite You Anally Retentive Hypochondriac You Hyperactive Megalomaniac You Dictatorial Piss-Pot and Arch-Prat...

While to the very best of my abilities executing my professional responsibilities in your company. And putting them to the fore.

Forty-Three

Dozing, half past something, woken by the phone. Sam's voice, plastered, broken: Hello, Are You Alone. Rowena's Gone And Done A Bunk. No Note Explanation Message. Can You Come Right Over.

I hear my own voice stumble over its Ohs and Noes. And put the phone down slow. Thinking: The one who matters most is always last to know. And mosey across town. CD deck tuned low.

Investment Fields. Manor Road. Guild Street. Mason Court. Templars Tower. Around Chevalier Circus and across Mortmain Square. Dogging the musty evening with its stale scent of October

Down Pain Lane cruises my green Primavera, intersecting the dark. Headlights spray plane trees yellow and patch iodine stains on their bark. And dead leaves flail at the spike-tipped rails

Of Eldorado Park. Along Alienation Avenue I put my foot down fast. Past Destitution Mews. Failure Alley. Desolation Row. Past blocks without numbers or names. Shadows layered on shadows.

Cracked windows. Peeling frames. And on, into suburbia. Sterility Square. Subsidy Street. Paranoia Parade. Turn right down Anxiety Crescent. And third right again. Desirable Milton Drive.

To Hell With Her, blurts Sam, flinging wide the door. Eyes hollow, eyelids bloated. Am Glad The Bitch Is Gorn. Far Better Orf Without. Ho Me, The One-Night Stud. That Creep She's Run Orf With

Is Just A Third Class Wally. Help Yourself To A Whatnot Whatever. As If It Mattered Anyway. Plenty More Where That. Coz Now Nothing Matters. Sam Sammy old Boy, I sigh. Just let her go her way.

If she wants to come back she will. Then it's for you to say. He slumps into an armchair. Downs another scotch. Spits into his glass. Brays: I'm Bloody Useless Mate. Failed. As A Man. As A Male.

Two hours later: I really must be off Sam. Do pull yourself together. Back via Puritan Place. Imperial Way. Exploitation Boulevard. Past Hope Street (No Entry). And at last, Atlanta Road.

Forty-Four

Room 1409, Wellcome Hotel, Stratford-upon-Avon (England). In Service Motivation Programming, which is one of my specialties,

She said, is Wow Uplift with these conventions. Which is why I deploy my own expertise in the field, tough on my PA Bernie

Who is a guy overprone to analysis error or malfunction when marginally off-base, will you pass me that slim-line, she said,

Beaming at the ceiling. Careful please with that Fire Water near my contacts. If his creativity ratings drop any lower I may

Just delete Bernie, in room 1409, Wellcome Hotel, Stratford-upon-Avon (England). Her trouser suit, blouse, tights and look-no-brassière,

All recently vacated and now draped, crisp and businesslike on a red leathertone chair, made no statement, offered no further comment.

Neither did I. I lay between her legs, waiting, wishing her somebody else. I even thought of you, out there in the nude unknown,

Fully occupied under Nick, Tony, Taki, whoever. This game-play did the trick and turned on my inner screen

Activating usual images. A worn snake-charmer's pipe down my spine set its old cobra dancing in slow time to its whine

And somebody seemed to moan a little around the rim of the song. It wasn't you or me. Then the music slowed, dissolved,

And the heady serpent collapsed to lie coiled in its jar. And I heard nothing. Nothing. Until: I think you're kinda cute,

She sighed. But I guess this sex thing's gonna continue like problematic in the post-technic era maybe another coupla hundred years

Before we see any real results in the one-on-one interface arena. The reallest most productive consciousness-raising convention

I was deputed to by Amglo this current year was Hawaii Interfocus. Kinda strange your people didn't think to send you along.

Forty-Five

If I may make so bold as to speak. From outside the chair as it were. Here we go again. Sir Keith is wont to play Arthur. Charlie his yawn nigh smothereth. *If you would care to turn*

To page letmesee seventy-four paragraph four subsection (b) of memorandum in hand dated April twenty first thatistosay half way through section concerning relocation/deployment

Of personnel at Bristol branch to adapt our overall billing and PR system to alternative procedures posited by new downloading access modality installations between Head and Regional Offices . . .

Peter picketh his nose. He left his wife last month but his amour backtracked to hir housbonde. Now hee loketh pasty and groweth old and bald. Piero il poverone. Bandito abbandonato.

Rex whispereth to Stuart who gazeth down at hys blotto. Martyn mumbleth betimes. Sir Keith prepareth to parry. But Maurice shaketh his head and fiddleth with his stilo. Aye bristleth

His nether lippe and his lowe browe furroweth. Planneth hee yet to squeak already so soon. Indeed now squeaketh hee. *Really shouldn't that be dealt with under Item Six. I mean shouldn't it really*

Go under General Admin. Good ole Maurizio his verbal mouse hath delivered. Nauseating twerp grafting ambitious twit. Bold Charlie his snigger safe-catcheth. Hold, now the Fair Elaine,

Statutory Woman, approacheth the listes ful fetis, with speech cool crisp and even. The whole assemblage noddeth and smug gloat Sir Keith and Maurizio. Grazie alla bell' Eleanora

who championeth everich cause, the compaignye hath acknowledgèd without so much as a vote, ych gallant contestor true victor in this jostle. Elaine's buxom bosom quivereth through

Virtu of hir corsages. Under the table hir legges cross and uncross. I wonder what she'd be like. Slowly. From behind. Now upon me she bestoweth hir Confident Positive Smile. From

Beneath hir contact lenses. I fiddle in my pocket for my secret pack of filtres. Menthol Extra Mild. And burrow through the minutes for a lost particular item.

Some point to clarify I seem to have lost somewhere. A dim a dam a cad? Admin adman a plan? A mandate for? Mendacity? Amenity? Amen. Or maybe simply

A man? Hic Iacet Adam Kadmon? Something of that sort, at any rate. Whatever needs saying will get said by someone or other. Sooner or later. I very much doubt whether it will ever be me.

Forty-Six

This bed smells of Eleni Deirdre Jane. I wonder will they come again. Rest me in heart's ease. Relieve my pain.

And now you. With whom I find no peace or balm but struggle fear and longing

And question after question. Every one unanswered. My beautiful comrade my fellow my serene eyed Sherpa

From Highbury. Who on Sunday leadeth me up Parliament Hill. My Artemis of 99 The Grove (Golders Green).

Who at The Plough on Saturday drank six pints of Harvest. Then danced solo syrtaki till 2 at To Fengari.

My moonwalker psychopomp guide through weeping and laughter. In dreams when I see you, statuesque, towering,

Waving your rifle high, clambering in denim over the barricades, you call to me, ferociously, as I cower somewhere behind you,

Avanti il Popolo. Ελευθερία η θάνατος. Братство и јединство. Brûler Les Écoles. À bas le savoir bourgeois.

Forty-Seven

Once in bed you said, Shall we be buried together. I don't want to die before you. But couldn't bear life without you.

And another time you said: I'd like to curl up so tiny you could carry me in your breastpocket. Where I'd sit safe and warm

Listening to your heartbeats. And sometimes you'd take me out, stroke me gently, and talk to me. And another: I love you

From the deepest well of my soul. So deep inside me I carry you, that's why I forget to tell you things. I seem to think you know

All my thoughts already. And I lay thoughtful yet thoughtless, thinking, This is truth and wisdom. And, in case God might overhear,

Hey God, I laughed. If You're there, in all Yr Heavenly Glory, and haven't got Yr wires crossed, or aren't busy somewhere else,

And wd like rare praise from me, though vain and insignificant, do deign to glance down here one moment. Thank You for this woman

And for sharing her with me. Thank You for the gift of this giver. Who gives her own self. Truly. In mortal terror and danger.

Forty-Eight

Well this Adam Kadmon mate what's the name of his group. Don't you come yobboing me Charlie. You're the wrong side of town for that stuff. We can't have the likes of you

Talking to people like that. Disturbing all the neighbours. Offending bystanders and suchlike. You just ask Joe here. You could get yourself arrested. Using provocative language.

What's that you never. Look mate I heard what you said. Really Charles old boy really. I really am surprised at you. You want to be more careful. Watch your manners a bit.

Hey take a butchers at his trousers Joe aint they revolting. What you got inside them darling. A Curly-Wurly and two Creme Eggs. Bet you he's got a long one in there Joe.

Yeah to stuff up his own fancy arse. Nah he aint got nothing but jelly babies. Tucked up in cotton wool so they won't get bruised. *Oh leave the little wanker alone. Can't you see he's a poofter.*

Just a minute Joe. Get an eyeful of this outfit. Brown velvet well really I ask you. Bet you that lot didn't fall off of the back of no bleeding lorry. Did it eh ducky. I said

Did. It. Eh. Ducky. Hey you Mister Fancy Pants it's you I'm talking to see. Didn't no-one ever teach you. It's rude not to answer questions. Oh dearie me now who's a naughty little fellow

You didn't want to go and call a nasty old *policeman* did you. Think you can poncefoot it round this part of town looking like Peter frigging Pan. Coz you're on our beat now see. We

Protects the public round here. We keeps the dirt off the streets. So why don't you just. Be ever such a good. Little Charlie eh. And show us what. You've got. Tucked up in the pockets

Of those nice. Brown. Velvet. Trousers. Well fuck me Joe this fucking fucker won't fucking fuck up his fucking cash. I'll show the fucker what's what. Give him the one arm bandit.

Forty-Nine

My arms have been amputated. I am naked to the waist. I run to the chamber of showers to check myself in the mirror. Into each socket

Is plugged the trunk of a foetus. Limp head expressionless. Pin eyes and fish mouth shut. Fingers on each arm, like those of tree frogs,

Splayed and transparent. Suckers on their tips. Wencott, most expert bully in the whole third year, stands behind me sneering

Bags. Me. Teach. This. Rotten. Little. Runt. His Lesson. Didn't I. Warn You. Moronic. Creep. Not to. Snitch. Piglet. Off Me.

He flicks my back with his wet towel. Red wheals appear. I have no arms to defend myself. He keeps me turning twisting. Warily

I watch. He feints and evades me, dancing like a boxer. Aims his towel at my prick. Tugs my pyjama cord. My erection springs free.

Rex Maurice and Keith look on. They slouch against the basins wearing their usual suits. Maurice the sneak keeps KV by the door.

Keith leans on the windowsill, hands in his pockets, whistling. Oh Fains I Say Honestly You Fellows, desperately I stammer. Just

Give us a chance. Rex hums tunelessly and glances at his watch. Can't you get a move on Wencott, he frowns. We haven't got

All fucking day. I Say It's All Right Really Chaps, I beg. Look I can explain everything. Honestly I can. If you'll just give me extra time.

They exchange winks and glances. Cough and adjust their sprawls. We're afraid that's out of the question, drools Maurice.

We've another appointment in town Old Man. Rex splutters: Oh that's rich. Another appointment in town. Suddenly Keith whistles

And they all start clapping. Stomping. Roaring. Slapping. Kicking me to the floor. Turning all the taps on. Closing the door on me.

I just manage to stand. You Bastards, I scream. You Sods. Pounding my head on the door. I'm no different from you. I'm not I'm not.

Fifty

Hello. Hello. Are you there. Is that really you. What is the good of the traffic

The rushing to urgent meetings. The mortgages and bank loans. The research and the investments. The trees blossoming and fruiting. The in-tray and the out.

The percentages and bids. The train journeys to and from work. The car journeys to and from home. The gossip liaisons secrets. Mowing the growing grass.

The records signatures messages. The wavelengths and vibrations. The losses longings regrets. The weekends the flights the dreams. The bookings the tickets the seats.

The screens bars curtains panes. Le Quattro Stagioni. The borrowing the burrowing the prayers. The actual and imagined couplings. The new and the old machines.

When death will swallow us all. And we shall all go down. And our thoughts rots or burn with our bodies. And suffering never end. What is the good of the

Sorry. Sorry. Really, I thought you. Somebody else. Terribly sorry to have bothered. Wrong number. Sorry indeed.

Fifty-One

I sit behind my desk in a thick band of shadow. Your photograph
leans in sunlight against its cardboard prop

Facing me untroubled with your gone eyes, your lips half parted,
your high untroubled forehead, hair swept back in a bun,

Cheeks' too familiar texture and proud profile of neck and chin.
I cannot work or think. You have shattered this now entirely,

Flooded its pieces in echoes and blurred their edges and borders.
I turn the photograph face down and my gaze

Escapes through the window. But see you still clear in each object
my unfocused eyes drift over. You're reflected

In silvered panes of the office block over the street. You walk along
the pavement in the shape of another woman

Who enters the newsagent's and emerges wearing your smile, carrying your handbag and the paper you always read.

This is The Daily Mockery. There is no corner of anything does
not remind me of you. You have locked your image inside me

And thrown away the key. I wear it under my skin. I cannot dismiss
or banish it. I rot and shrink in your shadow.

When the telephone next rings I shall start from my swivelled chair.
Knowing whatever voice wants me will not be yours.

CURRICULUM VITAE

Galactic Open Vlet Champion three years running. Originator of opening gambit known as 'One Eyed Juggler over Yildrith'. Capped for Interzonal League a record 43 times.

Born in Mars's Bellona. Studied microtopology under Rowan-Robson at Lux on Iapetus. Learned baghlamà from Bellou III at the Vamvakaris Academy. With Bellou IV ('Koré'), toured two seasons

As lead tsiftetéli in her Black Ice Combo & Horo. Espionage Officer for the Moon Federation. Operating out of Iapetus throughout Neutrino War. Captured once but released after 48 hours.

Ransom sum officially withheld. Precise rank unspecified. Nature of intelligence work undivulged and unavailable from LunSec. No medals other than Neutron Star (standard service issue).

Returned to incognito in Lux's Unlicensed Sector. Underwent face surgery. Initiate of The Sygn (Order of Disks, 12th Grade). For 6 years observed pledge of silence but refused to live on Commune.

Re-emerged as major commentator on Ashima Slade's Shadows: Some Informal Remarks Towards the Modular Calculus (Harbin-y Lectures, University of Lux, Department of Hermeneutics):

JB-CV1/ PTO

c.f. 'An Approach to Approaching Shadows', in Foundation: A Philosophical Quarterly, LUP, Vol. 64, No. 2, pp. 279-381' and 'Logics of p Variables', ibid., Vol. 67, No. 3, pp. 507 ff.

Resigned professorship and fellowship. Member of celebrated Phasalist Group. Reputed to have inspired Ron Barbara's poems Syntax III, Themos and Ice/Flows. Corinda's masterpiece,

The opera Eridani, is dedicated to him. Holographic Institute records for this period show him in company with novelist Foyedor Huang Ding and actress-director Gene Trimbell. In his last years

Performed with Trimbell's Street Microtheatre, Lux. Best known for role in Exit, Pursued By A Bear. Died peacefully aged 97 in heterophilic Commune B-302 (bisexual) on South 44th in Unlicensed Sector.

JB-CV2/ FIN

Part Two

Fifty-Two

Last night I was kept awake by owls around the house. Screaming like demented women before or during rape. I thought I heard

Scraps of human conversation in and between their love calls. Married couples tearing each others' hearts out. Then silence.

Fifty-Three

Through the aerial arrival gate the summer clients flow. I stalk them like a punter. I track them like a hunter. The fellow I'm expecting is one I do not know. I chew my gum and wait. My cud of bile rises.

I bide and waste my time. I need to get back to the office. Really there's far too much I really should be getting on with. And this fucking pick up job's far too fucking far beneath a Person Of *My* Status.

I hold my card up bearing the alien name. Will I recognise him? What if we miss each other? Shall I be held to blame? I scan features fashions coats cuts styles. Quantities and qualities of luggage and hand luggage.

Then, in an enriched instant, anxiety cracks and flakes from me like a prickly carapace. And I lose myself in a sudden now that bears no rank title or mark of recognition. And has no end or beginning.

The languages, the languages that all these people speak! And variety of voices! Each the print of a Being – born, breathing and unique. I mean how *amazing* how *fantastic* to be a passer-by in Babel. Let alone to

Fly Club Class! With Fast Track Ticketing and Use of Priority Lounge! To be a Passport-Carrying Member of The Community Of Cloud! Never upon This World had I known life had unleashed so many.

For here, at this gate from the No-Man's Land of infinite possibilities. All rapidly disappearing headlong into oblivion. Isn't this where whatever 'I' is inexorably belongs? I hum a little song.

At this Terrestrial Entry Point the currents ebb and flow. Eddying to and fro. I watch them like a painter, like Michelangelo. And trace the name *Human* beneath identities on show. Now who can

This stranger be, proffering a hand. Oh, I was dreaming, atmospheres away. Floating unfettered in unadulterated day. Swathed in rays of sunshine at 3000 feet. Jesus it is a *Woman*. And by no means

Wow bad-looking. Big Smile Blue Eyes Bold Perfume. Gear chic, crisp, *soignée*. Oh Well Done Looie Laddie – Bravo and Hooray. *You Err Mistair Charles Jordan Bruno of Prosepicked*? Yes Indeed. And I find

Myself grinning, I Represent MAPLAN. You Must Be Madame Takhireva. From Kompas Takavstan. Or Is It Tavakstan. I Mean Hello. Hello. Our Chauffeur Is Outside Waiting. Welcome. Shall We Go?

Fifty-Four

Why you must to tell me these stories about other women, she said, with whom you make love in your own country. Are you so insecure of yourself. I am not interested of what you do. I do not want to know.

She covered her face with her elbow as her hand clutched her pillow. I lit a cigarette and reached for the Becherovka. Also you drink too much, she said. Never I have known man to drink so much like you.

When I was married, I heard myself drone. I used to deceive my wife. When we split up I made myself a promise. Always to be truthful. At whatever cost. I've had my bellyful of lies. Other people's and my own.

She turned her head and looked simply through me. You are real big idiot fool, she said. To believe this so noble rubbish. Or else you are small ignorant boy. You have understood nothing. Nothing.

It is *alibism* only, always to tell truth. Her eyes glazed then frosted. I love also my husband. But whole truth is too painful. And anyway, is impossible. How could I explain to him. Anything of this.

She threw both hands out as if to contain the room. Grooved wood shutters and walls. Prints of Macocha Gorge. Clothes everywhere. Her suitcase, my suitcase. Ashtray full. Duty-free, Stuyvesant Mild.

Her new blue cashmere scarf draped over a chair. French eau de toilette, large. Two bars of black Belgian chocolate. Red Label, half bottle. Żubrówka. Borovička. Lozovača. If I would be living with you,

She laughed. And pummelled my chest lightly to punctuate each word. You. Degenerate. Middle-aged. Western. Corrupt. Model. Of Decadence. We should be devouring each other in no time more than five minutes.

Spasibo Tovarish, I said. Sondruhu můj. Very much indeed. Silhouetted against the bedside lamp, the nipples on her long breasts spread out in glowing points. Now, I said, quietly. Let me look at you now.

She hugged the coverlet close. My body is too fat, she pouted. I do not anymore like it. I pulled the drape down. Our eyes met and held. I stroked her belly folds and stretch marks on her hips

And brushed lips on the white horizontal of her hysterectomy scar. Drahoušku můj štestí moje srdíčko moje milačku můj, she moaned. March snows were melting on the pine slopes outside our cabin.

Fifty-Five

A polythene green dragon. With wooden spine and wingbone. And joints made of plastic

Soars lark-like above Wodensbury. Protector of the fortress. Herald of spring. Sweet harbinger.

He dips and pirouettes. He parries pauses swoops. Now he is a falcon. He climbs a little higher. And now he's the spirit

Of Albion. Arising in conquest over the Heaths and Hills. Over the Thatches and Thatchers. The Whitehouses and Whitelaws.

Gladly he buffets the wind. He brings us honey tomorrow. He promises liberty. He makes our hearts sing.

Don't hold the strings like that, silly. Do you want to bring him down. Pull it, you nana. Pull the thing. Pull. Harder.

And Oh Dad, look. Just look at those ducks. And the baby ducklings too. Oh aren't they sweet.

Now you hold onto the strings and I'll sit down a mo. Yes lie back and watch the clouds. Oh a day like this is heaven

Except for the dead under grass. Whom always I hear weeping. And except for the children of the living dead. Who cry out

Now it's my turn Dad. Can I have my turn now please. He's had his. Dad oh Dad it isn't fair Dad.

Fifty-Six

The Saturday before they left I drove her into town. Parked in the multi-storey and went looking for a heart-shaped pendant. Nearly all the upmarket jewellers' were stuffed with high-class kitsch.

Finally, in a craft shop run by a local co-op, we found just the thing she'd wanted. She picked it out herself, unerringly, from the showcase. Pointed at it under the glass and said simply, That one.

A little silver locket, unengraved, unadorned. The kind of thing I'd have gone for too. Thank You Thank You Daddy, she kept on repeating. It's my specialest jewel and I'll love it for ever and ever. Then we drove

Back to the house, full of her mother's boxes. Cleared the living room table and sorted through old photos. Selected one of each of us. Cut out paper templates. And then around our heads. And carefully

Stuck the images into their silver spaces. The one of her with a background of sea at Margate last summer. The one of me, against Charles Bridge, with the River Vltava behind. Then Sunday afternoon

I took her for a walk on Wodensbury. Hills on the horizon bluish under racing clouds. Photographed her against reticent sheep, and snowdrop and aconite clusters. Early March, and too late for weeping.

Fifty-Seven

MEMO

To the Psychometric Testing Evaluation Unit, Human Resource Management and Planning Department:

Many thanks for providing me with yr In-House Voluntary Pilot Survey consisting of blandly worded and meticulously researched sequence of 100 multichoice questions and statements supplemented by further 50 gap-fills built on structurally interconnecting and integrated parameters carefully embedded in which

Lie questions you deliberately decline to highlight or otherwise identify and claim are not only able to detect outright lies and deliberately misleading statements in whichever set of answers may be given by any idiot who might mistakenly think it worthwhile having a go at pulling the wool over yr all-seeing infallible eyes

But will also guarantee accuracy and ensure an overall objective and thorough evaluation of the suitability of personnel for the roles they are currently undertaking within the organizational (z not s) structure in order to ascertain not only current job-descriptions and job-satisfaction but also to assess the viability of immediate and short-term future plans

Within the organization for rightsizing outsourcing reclassification and redeployment of human resources on a principled basis beneficial to all employees. I must confess that despite these claims together with all additional assurances in yr covering memo that all and any results of the aforementioned testing procedures will be respected as being

Thoroughly confidential and for the limited reference of experienced and vetted personnel within the Human Resources Department on sole condition they that have received prior written permission in triplicate from the MD Finance Director and HR Director and will be stored securely in a database under a passcode accessible only to those three

In order to ensure that information therein will on no account be used on any occasion or in any manner to support actions or policies of any kind on the part of current or future board members management or share- or stakeholders which might be detrimental to the welfare security or short or long-term career-prospects of individual staff-members

That yr explicit instructions in each case to 'mark the statement that is closest to your opinion and the statement that is furthest from your opinion' are entirely meaningless to me bearing in mind that not one single one of the aforesaid statements even remotely coincides with anything I think now or have thought ever or am likely to think in future

And these all being equally alien to me my first subjective response was to experience acute feelings of guilt confusion and fear followed swiftly by serious moral and ethical misgivings about the whole exercise combined with a sense of absurdity which then concatenated into Total Outrage. I therefore regret that I decline to submit myself to this test.

Fifty-Eight

There go the dead again. Wailing. Constantly I hear them. Even when not listening. Even in this blind side of the partition wall.

Giggling in the office during coffee break. Conversing on the tube at the other end of the carriage. Beneath your voice on the phone.

In a meths drinker's snore from a bench on Platform 8. Whispering through the stadium under the crowd's roar. Crackling through gaps

In The Ultimate in CD Hi-Fi Integration. Despite metal particle coating lasers and microchips. Like a horde of Hollywood extras

In a multi-million epic. Like patients interminably queuing in the long-term ward. Like camp inmates trudging into the chamber

Of showers. Like an army of giant ants endlessly on the move. From hole to hole. From cell to cell. Street to street. Block to block.

City to city. From one hell to another. Under the human buzz. Under the rattle of wheels. Under the traffic drone. Constantly I hear

The dead lamenting Jerusalem. Albion's most sophisticated hot-time swinger. Pretty brunette 34-24-35 wants to exchange ideas and photos

With men with big problems. Will also model for same. Enjoys Pyjama Parties/O/Vib/Blowi Fans. Your place or mine. London or anywhere.

That's when she's off-duty doing overtime on the side. Otherwise trusty PA to Sir Keith W Lawdon. Prospect's Chairman of the Board and

Re-elected Chief Executive. President of the CBI. Adviser to the Board of Trade. Who lives on Bishop's Avenue. And is worth at least six million.

Fifty-Nine

If I were to speak I'd call up the dead on a disused line. If I were to call

I'd tap every wire in the sea to hear the unborn crooning. Across this flak and feedback. Across the traffic drone.

It wouldn't matter who. Maybe even a woman. Daughter of a daughter. Maybe even a man

Touching his own shadow outside Hut 63. Face buried downward under Siberian snow. From this distance the drowned all look alike

Their gestures seismic to their companions only. And their names indistinguishable. Their breaths inaudible.

Their smell faint and distant. Of rotted seaweed.

Sixty

I lift myself from despair by saying No to myself. No I shout at shutters brick walls drainpipes gutters. No at pavements lamp posts shop-fronts passing cars.

No at blinds in windows net curtains geraniums cactuses. No at green death's heads that peer through windows grinning. No at my own reflections under yellow lamplight.

No out of my head in half a dozen pubs. No at this bar filled with strangers on the wrong side of this city. No at daffodilled gardens and garages with two cars.

No as I reel home and stop on Atlanta Road Bridge. No at a passing train at girders planes new flats. No at signs barking Private No Entry One Way Keep Out.

If No could change history I'd dial God and tell him my No. Hey You there God I'd tell him. No to this pile of rubbish. No to tomorrow's promises lies the same as today's.

Goodbye little wife. Goodbye children. It is time at last to set sail. The blackest sea calls me. My gear is packed and ready. I shall not return with the sun.

No I sing. Nonny No. Not much of a beginning. If only You could hear me. If You'd just turn back the clocks. Ach what is the good of this. I have not opened my mouth.

Sixty-One

And if I were to greet you with my whole voice evolved and empty. As ready to be occupied as a cello or a hive.

You wouldn't hear them howling. You wouldn't track their silences. You wouldn't need to fear them under the traffic drone.

Nor would they stand weeping. The dead and the unborn. Knocking at our window at 2 o'clock in the morning. If I were to speak to you

Out of my whole origin. We wouldn't be neighbours only. Nor surreptitious lovers. We should be comrades sworn

Into the heart of the buried dream continent. Rowing down a single Nile into a shared Africa.

If I were not afraid. And afraid of my own fear. To speak. Of their howling and their silences. They would be one with this voice.

Can you hear me. Can you hear. As fearless as. Damn. The pips are going. But I haven't finished yet.

Sixty-Two

To say Mummy again. To call for you in the night. Between pillow-muffled howls in flight from wolves or bears

Who rise like ectoplasm every time I pass. Who balloon from cracks in the pavement. Who wait. Who threaten to jump.

And to find you there by the bedside. To swallow your soothing voice. Your fingers pouring currents that rinse pain away.

To slide between your arms like a fish in a deep ocean. To suck at your huge breast clawing with baby nails.

I stand erect supporting your corpse on my shoulder. The whole century is soaked in your blood.

Sixty-Three

Snowfall, two feet, at Green Hedges. Sole road to village impassable. And how many hours you sat there, who will ever know.

In Rowena's green Volvo. In the drive of your bungalow. Radio on low. On what wavelength – that's what I'd like to know.

Cigarette pack on lap, open. Scotch bottle, drained, by your side. Belt strapped. Choke out. And a green plastic garden hose

Taped from exhaust into air duct. The morning milkman found you. Head slumped sideways. No lights. Petrol tank empty. So

We got into the house forcing the back door. On the kitchen floor the miaowing cat had dragged in a broken-necked bird.

Fresh ash in the grate. Letters, maybe. And, cryptic, in the old typewriter, your note, in lower-case, initialled like a memo

```
for what I am about to do nobody else is responsible other
than me. i just couldnt take any more pain.
```

And that was all to tell. The house, veiled, muffled, white, in its wintry, country quietness. Quite clueless, spotless, innocent,

As if waiting, absurdly, prepared for your return. And Rowena said, God I never imagined you dying. Sammy you bloody fool

You said I was a tough old bitch. But now you've got me crying. You and your damn perfection. Even when you were lying,

Efficiency, control. Now you've really gone and got your perfection totally perfect haven't you. May God forgive your soul.

And later, in the morgue: Yes, this is him. I know my poor darling I know. In two feet of snow. Nowhere else to go.

Sixty-Four

The car turning the corner threatens my life with its growls. What stops it crashing through my skull

Is merest brick and mortar. Every sound of night breaks against these walls like glass. Outside the wind whirls rubbish

Leaves and newspapers. Dead. Footsteps on the pavement crackle like bonfires. Closing time voices

Pound on my ears. To the shelters. Get down below. Isn't that what they're shouting.

I pull the blue striped duvet higher over my head. The neighbour's hi fi groans. Some Enchanted Evening.

Water pipes rattle and the cold tap drips. The boiler sings falsetto. The alarm by the bed patters its SOS.

Sleep is a monster who tortures before devouring. Through every home in town mounts the rising tide.

The telephone rings and rings. I will not answer it. Though it says, You're not dead yet but we're waiting for you baby.

Sixty-Five

I have spent much of my time looking for a small piece of joy I seem to have lost somewhere. Maybe in early childhood.

Like the jigsaw piece I dropped there. And it wedged between floorboards. And trying to prise it out I pushed it further in

And heard it drop between rafters. And splintered my right forefinger. And with a stolen needle extracted the woodsliver

And did not flinch or call but grinned at my squeezed blood drop. And for that adult grimace

Under gritted milkteeth, the loss of that wedge of innocence, my last cardboard clue to complete

And seal perfection – seemed small price, seemed nothing. Till now my strengths numb me. My silences conspire against me.

My secrets bar me out. My grin tortures my soul. I am least at home in my home. Memories erode my vision. And I am sick with longing

To stride back into that house. Obtain present owner's permission. Pull up his carpet and underfelt. Wrench his floorboards up

And find that missing fragment of dusty cobwebbed cardboard. With its faded bit of picture

Of sail and sea on its good side. And wear it on a chain in a locket. And treasure its golden presence.

But I have dredged the dream and lost the address of that child. Hey whatsyourname. Can you help. I can't remember. As usual.

Sixty-Six

What I have lost is perpetual and won't open flower or flesh to me, will not be prised apart, just clamps fast its bivalve shell, buried under memory's seafloor, disguised as a grain of sand.

Hey, I call. Come back. You I glimpse through summerhaze. You friend you darling you comrade. You I once knew better than now I know myself. You I trusted completely

Soul on my tongue tip. You, other. Complement, revealed. Blown presence of flowering gardens. Grey eyes flecked green. Face half forgotten. My dusty winged angel

How where and wherefore gone. Come in now. Come in please. Hello, is that you. Operator, I tap. I wonder if you can help me. I think I must have lost the one address I need

The city house street number. Mislaid the name note word. The clue key chord time tune. There must be some kind of code or combination lock. I can't find my compass and bearings

Though I did look for them, honest. But don't know my next move. Nor can I read these particular stars. This dazzle blocks them out. There's too much interference and

Somebody else on the line. I think it's another SOS and whoever it is says he's drowning. That we'll all go down together. Hello are you still there I think we've been cut off. But I call

Into a hollow conch a whitened bony spiral. And hear my own breath rasp as it calls me back to my self. Not what is lost, is perpetual. Not my dead voices, or whispers of waves on seabreeze.

Sixty-Seven

I have searched all over this house. Through lobby lounge and loft. Between leaves of books. In every cupboard and closet. Even behind mirrors. I have dredged the dream and the day. For you who were

Wholly perpetual are traceless as melted snow. Gone companions of honour from fastnesses of my kinghood and farthest regions of radiance, you who were angels once with no dust specks on your wings,

Where are you. Come back. You, last lost jigsaw piece dropped under infancy's floorboards. Deeper than a dandelion rooted between two pavement slabs. And I guilty of cutting off your head.

And you, crayoned paper clown. Giant taller than cedar or redwood to me. My dragon and monster slayer. And best dream defender. Your spiky blazoned smile and bright hair burnt to ash.

And you, my brave lead warrior. My proud plumed grenadier. Who sank into our garden pond. Due to report back to surface tied to a piece of string. Whose cable snapped in that nether world. Where still you lie drowning.

And you, silver cufflinks inherited from my father. Gone AWOL when I last looked in your red leather box. And a gong hammer hit my heart and went on resounding through. For I'd clambered

Onto his lap and toyed with you at his sleeve ends. And said. Daddy. When you die. What will happen to these. And he'd laughed and said. My Son. Whatever I have. I promise. One day will be yours.

Hey you, I call. Gone presences: now figments dulled in camouflage or, varnished, shells and shards, well meshed into the backgrounds of things: your shapeless glimmers and reckonings, your screens

And unbeckoning blindspots, your silent desert valleys and sheen-scratched patches of mist: unhuntable chameleons, what language do you speak these days, who lived through so many forms: each hallmarked

Perfection. Aren't you there, I call. Angels. Won't you please come in now. But my line to the dead has been permanently disconnected. No sound comes back from the pillow or interceding dark.

Sixty-Eight

Sir. Since the living are flesh-enmeshed, the dead cry out to be heard. They paint summer rose. They groan

Through creaking trees. They bleach the stars in dawn. They dye evening henna. They place sweet-smelling suns

In a pot of herbs by our gate. Against earth and water they wrestle upwards constantly. To hatch, in nests of fire,

Song exhumed from glaciers. That it float free, from the seafloor's sandy and rocky wastes. To surface

On the mind's waters and walk its waves like angels. Before dispersing on air. Like memories. Like dead leaves.

To evaporate, banked in clouds. And through wind blowing low on the mountain I know in dreams they may speak.

Wittering or babbling in their alien tongues. Or prophesy in wordless riddles

Although precisely, through music. And, most rare even hint, obliquely, at action: *Six in the first place means*

No blame on the departed. It furthers one to travel across the Great Water. Danger at the outset. At the end, success.

All this I know. Always I hear their soundings. And have even traced and followed their singular texts. But what they mean

Falls unknowable, lies permanently hidden, dark even in purest whiteness, melts light as passing snow. Therefore

Thank you for yr enquiry. Regret Tues & Weds out. Kindly arrange alternative appointment

Thurs. Sir Keith Wallace Lawdon, Chairman of the Board, is fully booked this week. But Ms. Gemma Hussey,

Company Sec of one of our subsidiaries (Mann Rogers & Greaves) will be available to see you

2.00 p.m. Thurs. Wd you kindly confirm by return. Assuring you of all our etcetera etcetera.

Thanks. Kindly barred in senses five. Thanks, armed in good intentions. Thank you

Cordially, faithfully. Oh thank you, sincerely, following the heart's pathetic beat.

Sixty-Nine

Here my darling is the house I've had specially built for us. A wooden chalet on stilts. To protect it from snakes and spiders. With a horseshoe over its door.

Do you think we should name it Sweet Yoke. Or maybe Fair Bridal. I honestly think you should choose. To me it is pure perfection. And now, since it's May and noon

And we have bathed and dressed. And you've performed sunny ablutions. With soap oil powder creams. And brush comb and drier. And smell and look quite divine.

And white blossoms blow through our windows. And the blackbird brags in our hedge. And bluebells and wild pansies bloom richly in the woods. And tulips in our garden. It is time

For a stroll outside. Where just around the corner who should we meet but Nicholas. Who sits as if waiting. Puffing on his pipe. Parked in his white MG with personalised number-plates.

I prepare for polite magnanimity. For affable nonversation. But your steps quicken. Very slightly. He glances at his watch. He gets out of his car. He says

Hello. Are you ready. Your tongue tip touches your upper lip. You curl your left toe inward. You look quickly down. Your eyes blaze blue green fire. Yes you say. I'm ready.

And as in one complex dance figure rehearsed a thousand times. To reach its point of perfection at precisely this instant. Too bitterly beautiful. And never to be repeated.

He opens the passenger door you climb in sit down fasten your safety belt he walks round the bonnet to take his driver's seat you wind down your window look up

What's happening, I whisper. What are you doing for God's sake. Now your voice shakes too. Thinly veneered with control. I've decided to go with Nick. And now we'd better be off.

I don't understand, I blather, Darling. Please. I love you. Are you trying to break my heart. This isn't real. Please, you say mutely with eyes and lips. Oh please please don't.

But you just can't do this, I burble. It can't be true. It's not happening. We're everything together. What shall I do without you. That's entirely your affair, you weep, as his car pulls away.

Seventy

Chill east wind from Poland interrogates all I own. Threatens to sever skin from flesh. Flay nerve from bone. I cross absent landlord's yard and pull up his garage door. Climb in new blue Mondeo

And purr into Gravesend. Mission: fish and chips from shop on Darnley Rd corner. Accomplished: steer back towards digs on Singlewell Rd. Greasy packet stinks on empty seat beside me. Then I remember

November 5th. Threepoint turn in a sidestreet and back into town. My breath condenses on windscreen. Up steep Shrubbery Rd. Onto Windmill Hill. Plenty of parking space. I've left it too late. As usual.

The bonfire has burnt low. Clumps of parents and children still stand knotted and wrapped in the glow. Two ten year olds light sparklers and twirl them. Like Moebius strips, in white figures of eight.

A girl says, Why don't the rockets work properly this year Mum. Over the river in Essex the lights of Tilbury blaze. That looks like a big ship docked there, says Dad. Could it be the Stefan Batory

Soon to move down river. Past Canvey Sheppey Shoebury. Back to Gdansk or Gdynia. Or over to Toronto. And is Dad thinking, like me: I doubt I shall ever sail in her. Upstream red lights top the chimneys

Over the cement works. Mum says: Time we had an outing. Up to Greenwich and The Tower. One weekend in Spring Oooh Can we Can we Please Dad. The girl jumps up and down. Behind me stretch The Downs

Pilgrim's Way Happy Valley. I return to a cold house. Rented. To fish and chips. Also cold. Turn on gas fire. Watch Wednesday Western. The West is lost or won. Bleeding coloured shapes on the screen

Like withered tree stumps in Hades. While down by the river before me. Half a mile away. Sleeps Princess Pocahontas. Whom no fire shall reawaken. And my children two hundred miles away. In another city.

Seventy-One

Nobody calls. The whole house is silent. But my head is on the autobahn. With slipways to sea and mountains. Is this the way

To Trieste. Trst Tryst Truth Truce Twist Trust. Or the blue fringe of numbness between madness and impossibility. Where the brain

Swills final storms before its last signal stills. Before the highway kills. In migraine, mind-tempest, unreason. World, frogskin

Of a pierced balloon, where is your swell horizon. On the whitened edge of silence the stars go out one by one. The big beginning

Of time has clanged for good, doubly bolted. What is beyond is mist. Gone lips I have kissed. Burned to gold. Turned old.

Can these be the keys my keys. From standstill ignition clutch handbrake to gas. And from first into top gear to death.

Seventy-Two

The minister has been tainted. When his wife was told, she fainted. Yes I do suppose it's *possible* he's not the monster he's painted.

Our consciences are a riddle. Look, who *isn't* on the fiddle? The pole across the abyss sags to breaking point in the middle.

The emperor has lost control. This country leaks, like a cracked bowl. *So get thee into exile, mate, and try to save your soul.*

Seventy-Three

He chats to me cheerily outside the porch of his villa. But of course you can see her Old Chap, he smiles. You don't need my permission. He swells with magnanimity. I wince as his hand pats my shoulder. She's a perfectly free agent here.

He surveys his white veranda with its mammoth baysize view. Its thick unscaleable walls with bougainvillea blooming. Its sunbed cushions awnings and well-stocked cocktail cabinet. And in the pebbled drive his two white cars parked carelessly. So do come on in

And join us for a quick drink Do. She'll be delighted I'm sure. I grind my teeth and smile. And follow him through his thick piled halls hung with expensive originals. Outside a glass door he pauses, a forefinger over his smirk.

Naked over the ironing board, you never looked more beautiful. I stand admiring speechless. A smile plays familiar scratchy tunes on the left corner of your mouth. I remember every inch of you. My lips and throat parch. I swallow numb to speak.

Our eyes meet and leap. Steady and immediate. Blaze blue green fire. Both our entire lives till now pass through each other's this instant. I know. I know you know. We open our mouths and neither says a word. Memories drain away.

Darling, says Mein Host. Just for old time's sake. A demonstration for whatsisname. He perches and unzips. Your gaze shifts to him slowly you put your iron down you kneel before him expressionless your eyes meet mine then glaze.

Oh stop this now, I roar. Nicholas looks up surprised. Is anything the matter Old Chap. Just hang on a tick would you. Then I'll pour you that drink. You suck lick etcetera your head bobs up and down. He murmurs groans and slouches against the wall.

You squat on the floor retching. You gasp and wipe your mouth. Oh God Oh God, I moan. And now you breathe stand grimace. Clench fists eyes teeth. And spit: Wasn't this what you wanted you nasty little swine. So now you've really seen it

You can get right out of here. You'll get no more turn-ons from me. This is my life not yours. I do what I like with it. I'm not an extension of you. So stop prying and spying on me. And please be so good. As not to come back here. Ever.

Seventy-Four

Adam Kadmon hangs upside down in the Sistine of my skull. My poor damned Cad Man. MacPaul Muhadman Cabman. My ole pal Hangman Camden. Mein pale Haridan Gottman. Hung batter than any vamp.

How oft did I climb scaffold ladders aloft to the roof of her cave. I could scalpel her there with my palate knife, my tongue screwed into her rafters. My reddened beat rooting verily for the Crux of the Mater,

That she might deign to take my matter in hand. Whine knot, if you insist, she positively cooed. Only if you encyst. And neath her waste did I wrack, for'ard and back, for my knead lay strong upon me.

Gwynny My Lombard Schwarzkopf (somhwat like that I'd moan), For thee would I souse and toast and leave this world's sick scene, regodless of its myriad pettiful schmontradictions. And I, only I, in my villa

In Valhalla, your simple Launcelot. Nay sooth indeed Milord, she cogitatively pooed. Just coz I prance a lot. Thou'rt suffering from postmature gesticulations, venial depretensions and laud nose hwat

Other hoo-ha. 'Ere lemme take thy pulse. Och dost know hwat. Rotten chance oust gotten unless th'art operated. Now don't worry lovie, for I'll abride with thee. And twat then, My Madam, My Raw Dam?

No longer trouting me, into her whispry cauldron whistled maw stunty infantry. Seamed tight in her steamy cavern, baubled in her marrow coven, she bearded Sir Keith, Rex, Maurice, Taki, Sam, Antonio

And who else lewd nose. She polished their flaws with her towel. She spaded their foils knightly. She lollipopped rake hoe and trowel. Yet me, she merely owlhooted: Mate, git thee gorn away. Whence I,

Sir Loin Cup, Sur Cur de Leon, Sir Cutlet Stake, by Sour Custard Lake, a loon and malely loitering, now sick of bland bands and wagons, must speak of hands and bygones, and comfort me with flagons,

Festering, caulked in cowardspeak nella Capella della Solitudine, spieling my unluck in turning, stiff brailling my sour stuff, back burning, unrealing my track, unreturning. Where no birds ding-a-ling.

Seventy-Five

Cedar Ward. Beech Ward. Oak Ward. Ash Ward. This is a real place. The nurses also are real. To prove it they don't wear uniforms.

You can come and go as you please. A garden inclosed in my sister. Under semi-narcosis.

And when she came out of it she said, I'm Hitler's wife. So the nurses put her in a linen smock. And shut her in a padded room. Sleep

O gentle sleep. And when she came out of that she screamed and bit the nurses. And overhead up grew

Insuperable highth of loftiest shade. So the nurses gave her electroconvulsive therapy. And she quietened down a bit.

A garden is my sister. Her head enclosed in barbed wire.

Seventy-Six

Damnedness and madness. Higher onto sleephill I trycrawl. I crytrawl

Calfing in my own blood. But never itch to the top. I will I want I wish I need I fail. Three a. m. How can my amhead

Let go my itflesh. How can the gaoler free the prisoner without abode-orders.

Hope-rope to justice pinnacle! To umblivion! To wisdumbness! I want you around my waste. But you tie tomb pound

Lead waits around this my neck I hang from. I missed her. Oh must err. Of my fishbait. My corkfloat. My mandeath. You

Catch me on your lank importal line. You tear my tongue out. You trout-hook me to sky.

Seventy-Seven

This is a Reassessment Unit as well as a Deselection Centre. In this section, you may see The Mothers. Observe through this one-way panel into the Holding Room. Don't worry, they can't see us. They've no idea we're watching.

See how they line the walls. As if clinging for support. Not one stands in the centre. Observe the posture of shoulders. No, we certainly do not supply our patients with benches. Unnecessary luxury. Take up much-needed space.

That one's boy is dying of leukaemia. Aged a mere seventeen. And she a Yakut diamond heiress. With a triple-tier penthouse with mezzanine overlooking Centennial Park. Plus villa with blue- bottomed swimming pool on the brink of Monte Capriccio.

See that one, on the left? Tall, gaunt-faced, hollowed back? Now, her son has been sectioned. Just after receiving his Cambridge doctorate. Research on homeomorphy in mammalian bone structures. Spent last summer sleeping rough

Across the length and breadth of England. Police picked him up in Dunwich listening for nightingales. Said he was looking for the city of Ys, drowned under salt and foam. As for the mother – she has turned to seed, to seaweed.

And here is yet another rather hopeless case. She recognises no-one. Observe the whites of her eyes. Yellowing, bloodshot, cracked. Like old porcelain in a junk shop. Her son was a squaddie or something. Served in the so-called Peace-Keeping Force

In former Ludoslovakia. Or was it Severoslavia. Or Krudistan. Or Bruanda. What difference does it make. Along some fissure, at any rate, on some ethno-religious timewarp. Of course these are mere samples of the range of patients we treat and of services

We offer now at this very moment in time within our professional care. Yes indeed. They are all of them waiting. Who for. For me, of course. Nurse, call in the next one. Where is that idiot hag. Have you gone bloody deaf. I said, Nurse, Call In The Next.

Seventy-Eight

Hip Know sissies knot holy rill Eyeable laser Tree torment, unknotter beet Ryed dick's Apt ink Aces lie come Knee easier or ratter Axe eyore, Jew Sea,

Sadder Dock to Pay shunt lea. And Judas plain Eye thereof air Tip pickle Sets us Imp Thames. Butcher Mussed righter Wrest a bitch, yuh No

Weave Die egg Nosed ass Haiku matty con Dish hunk cold Hiss tory list ness, witches dee Finders Toe cull Lucker Reel eyes Asian 'em piss Pecked Yvonne

Then Asses airy pearl It tickles sit you Asian Pro Veil him frew Awl Sicked as of 'em Asses, a Swellers ink Lasses prow Fission a lamb manna Jeery all.

So ferrous Wean Owe, er Come plucks Ken Own lea bee Reel leak Concord if fix Left Outer the Fool. Soya Mist Writer Pulley Tinter yes Sent err

Ant Ring kit Down toadied Rags. Eye muff Raid Udder wisers knotter Grater mounter bee Dumb ferret. Its quieter Come on Malaysian

Hotter beet Tucan Sirened dub out. Know wall Tern nut if, Jew Sea, butter Fay sin tether Darker Pro chin, amp Red you Dis dunk White Tinner saintly,

Unfine doubt what tits Seek retames aren't Twat tit Olds few. Isle Pitcher on try sigh click Ant he deep Press ants Two. Thee Own leak Your Real lea is Pay shunts.

*Hypnosis is not wholly reliable as a treatment, and
   not to be tried except in cases like amnesia or
   ataraxia, do you see,*

*Said the doctor patiently. And you display neither
   of their typical sets of symptoms. But you must
   try to rest a bit, you know.*

*We've diagnosed a psychosomatic condition called
   historylessness, which is defined as total lack of
   realisation and perspective*

*On the necessary political situation prevailing
   through all sectors of the masses, as well as in
   classes professional and managerial.*

*So far as we know, a complex can only be really
   conquered if it's lived out to the full. So you
   must try to pull it into your centre*

*And drink it down to the dregs. I'm afraid otherwise
   there's not a great amount to be done for it. It's
   quite a common malaise and*

*Not to be too concerned about. No alternative, do
   you see, but to face into the dark approaching,
   unprejudiced and quite innocently,*

*And find out what its secret aims are and what it
   holds for you. I'll put you on tricyclic anti-
   depressants too. The only cure really is patience.*

Seventy-Nine

FROM: PHONE NO.: 01217435677   Feb. 29 2000   01.00AM P1/2

Fax: URGENT

To: Prospect International Managing Director & Board of Directors

From: G Bruno alias J Dee alias P della Mirandola alias S Zevi.

With reference aforementioned item *Joy* believed by me personally mislaid somewhere in early childhood regret cannot state accurately time date place of loss or mode or exact circumstances thereof

Whether by disappearance metamorphosis theft burglary or other form of misappropriation by noxious agency or person or persons unknown with or without prejudice or other unspecified cause whatsoever

Since motive for such seems inexplicable according to both commonsense and all cited interpretations of relevant research into cases documented both pathological and nonpathological bearing in mind

Nontransferability of asset in question without conscious awareness subliminal suspicion or at least peripheral registration of exchance hangover or sobstitution progress on part of current incumbent

Nor can I anywhere find nor have in my possession relevant receipts invoices checkstubs card statements vouchers deeds warranties or other proofs of purchase or documentation of lease or ownership

And since none of my ongoing policies specifies coverage for such risk factor or eventuality under any clause or subsection nor indeed could be interpreted as likely to do so by any competent assessor

29-FEB-00   01217435677   P1/2

FROM : PHONE NO. : 01217435677   Feb. 29 2000   01.00AM P2/2

I have filled in no claim forms filed no police reports made no complaints signed no petitions but carried on as usual attempting without misdemeanour or disturbance to keep my affairs in order

Wherefore being of sound cheer fit disposition and according to current modes in my rightful mind am prepared to accept sustain and undertake to fulfil total responsibility and liability for said loss

Provided and on sole condition you guarantee full acknowledgement that I have made every possible attempt effort and investigation in my power to effect full recovery of aforesaid item notwithstanding

Recurrent partial amnesia absence pain rancour rage paranoia depression despair despondency grief guilt regret fear of death of dying loneliness numbness and all their common concomitants and physical

Symptoms and syndromes in their whole range of manifestations. Should this information involve contract cancellations tender withdrawals or suspension of or hindrance to any aspects soever of our hitherto

Cordial and mutually beneficial collaborations please advise forthwith. I hope however adequate alternative or failing that at least surro-gate arrangements can be made for satisfaction of all concerned parties.

Bruno
NAPALM Floating Manager Mddx
Prosepicked National

Eighty

We thought things might get better but it all deteriorates. The relevance of the utterance and the sincerity of the sayer.

The efficacy of law and the rites of pomp or prayer. The perishing rainforests and the hole in the ozone layer.

The spirit grows no wiser and the tongue excoriates. The furniture of the intellect is rickety and threadbare.

The fickle, sickened soul nightly confronts despair. While the wizened heart cries out, *Is there no-one to love out there?*

Eighty-One

After betrayal and after bereavement. After nights of panic and weeping. And their small hours spent rotting and shrinking in shadows. Worn by *ūhtcearu*, the Grief Before Dawn.

As summer's summit weighted on gardens. With falling of first plums and pears in our gardens. While straw was baled out of harvested fields. And burnt stubble blew through suburban windows.

Come, you said, North. In my small white Renault. Come, away from loss and despair. I'll do the driving and you'll read the map. We'll head for The Peaks and stay overnight

In a cheap B&B. I know we're both broke but what does that matter. I mean something simple. Nothing too fancy. Let's phone for a booking and make up a picnic. We'll both derive comfort

From the year on the turn. And the place. And old friendship. I sense I begin to find self-acceptance. Of a new kind. I can't quite explain. I mean new ways to live

Now middle age is real. I rejoice in the beauty of children and young folk. Hope blooms through their pores. From their speech. In their eyes. And I can consent, unjealous, to this.

And in Ye Derwent Hotel that night I too consented. You surprised me. You took me. You opened your body. Through your sadness and warmth you received me in. Dark eyed black haired woman

Who might be my own half-sister or cousin. Secret granddaughter of my forefathers' fatherings. Showed me the store of years I'd disparaged. Returned sight in my right eye.

Eighty-Two

This limestone cavern has the hugest mouth in England, grinned our guide as he led us into darkness. Though some politicians could probably compete. Its entrance is known as The Devil's Arse. Ladies, please

Pardon my French. And here, where the roof always drips, is Roger Rain's House. On that ledge, see The Orchestra, where locals gave chamber concerts and once entertained Queen Victoria. Poor Prince Albert too.

Passing this here tunnel we stoop seventeen yards. So hold on tight to your partners and watch it if you got lumbago. Now this stream we're crossing here is The Original River Styx. Notice how sudden the air

Grows chiller even than sorrow. In winter this whole passage is blocked with ice solid. In spring sudden floods engulf it to the roof. The air is rich in oxygen although in deathly darkness and will cure all manner of ailments

Arthritis sclerosis bronchitis colitis to name but a small selection. Monster pipistrels glide here and gorge on human flesh. Look there goes one now. Nearly lost your husband there didn't you madam. And these

Stone pillars is known as The Five Arches. Standing indeed a full half-mile from the cavemouth. Two more miles is mapped but nobody has dared go down deeper. This is where we turn back, kindly keep close together.

Smiling we held hands and followed him back into day, through rank moss and fern smells to leaves, grass and light. And, south past the quarry, drove to the moor edge. Freed of ghosts. Identifying our shadows.

Eighty-Three

Through heathered acres we tramped the moor, off marked paths, till, among sheep grazing, like canny, moving statues,

We came on the stone circle: bees and crickets whirred, whites and red admirables flittered, and some benevolent spirit,

Protector of that place, caught us suddenly shivering in each other's arms, although it was warm still, late summer,

And on a stony knoll, remains of a burial barrow, tipped us into wordlessness, and tumbled us laughing down

Into a grassy hollow invisible to the hills, where we joined smiles and, consenting, as if to one shared volition,

Came naked and knowing together, in a binding which unbound and shocked us both into recall

Of further scopes of years, layered, unwasted, innocent, still not for-med for reflection, hardly yet even warmed,

And our parched pasts unwithered, and hopes rooted in their place to grow new, possible cells

For future leafing and blooming in zones out of cognition; and walking back to your car

Across burnt heather patches that left soot-marks up to our knees, we found the old pathway,

And followed its half-buried track, not on your map, or mine, picking

Huge heather clumps, waists deep in purples, mauves, greens and golds.

Eighty-Four

I have tried to make sense of my life. Have kept my affairs in order. Observed control and decorum in all matters public. Never asked for perks. Not been too pushy. Driven within limits. Discreetly concealed expenses in legitimate tax concessions

Kept spreadsheets straight. Kept the in-tray clear. Infallibly chosen the right tie. Not tying too showy a knot. Sounded neither too officious nor too forward on the phone. Skied in the Alps and The Dolomites. Toured The Rhine The Loire The Rhône. Not to mention The Ardèche. And The Isère.

Invested in Hocks and Moselles of recommended vintage. Choosing one to uncork occasionally for a respected client. Or guest. Properly insured assets professional and otherwise. Kept careful tabs on cashflow. Kept hidden keys in triplicate for indispensable locks.

Filed papers alphabetically every weekday evening. Done press-ups pullups pushups each weekday morning. Jogged around the block. Game of squash on Saturdays with Rex or Maurice or Keith. Round of golf every month or so. To keep my membership up.

Carefully consulted with colleagues immediately senior and junior. Never rushed implementation after making and taking decisions. Always keen for frank discussion. In open democratic committee. Obtained planning permission from relevant subdepartments

While pumping their proper channels and keeping their clichés clear. Respected health hygiene and safety at work. Scrupulously maintained closets and cabinets. Offices air-conditioned. Trousers correctly creased. Linen freshly laundered. My own home doorstep spotless

With regular changes in personal secretary. Never pried too deeply into subordinates' private lives. Though taking a quick dip in the typing pool now and then. But for light refreshment only and not on an ongoing basis. To show a fitting concern for staff

Motivation morale and welfare. Foster competition. Encourage long-term loyalties. Maintain corporate efficiency at optimum not maximum output. Prevent energy waste while remaining urbanely humane. Conserving warmth in winter. Saving water in summer. Never throwing away

What might come in handy later. Albums of old invitations and programmes of plays. Snaps of college contemporaries and family holidays. Old school rugger fixture lists. With full details of scores. And an address book for contacts. Even if crashing bores.

Eighty-Five

Sir Keith Lawdon Dubai

From:	"Rex Harmer" <rex.harmer@prospect.com>
To:	Sir Keith Lawdon
	"Dubai" <fassbinder.suite@galaxyhotel.com>
Sent:	1 March 2000 09:34
Attachments:	brunofax.doc
Subject:	Bananas

Hello Keith,

Sorry to trouble you with this but to judge by his fax (see attachment) Bruno appears to have gone bananas. Will try to contain problem but may need to consult you for directions. Can you send contingency instructions. Thanks.

Rex

Eighty-Six

All the people I need to talk to seem to be unavailable. They've just popped out of the office. They've been moved on to another department. They've been shunted off to work in some exclusive subsidiary. They're on an outside assignment. They've been winged or booted upstairs. They've gone away on holiday. They're in an urgent meeting and cannot be disturbed. They're getting down to brass tacks and the real nitty gritty. They've just been redesignated or redeployed

To downsizing or downloading or decommissioning or deregulating. Or re-visioning or revaluing or resourcing or recycling. Or empowering or hot-desking or outreaching or leveraging. Or marketing or mentoring or monitoring or manhunting. Or stripping suspending liquidising freezing assets. Or venturing networking headhunting troubleshooting. Or evaluating new premises or commandeering global niches or transferring technologies with top know-how and expert follow-through

They're engaged in risk-assessment and crisis-control alternatives. They're formulating and calculating effective mission statements. They're critiquing client loyalty. They're second-guessing competitors' crass or cunning counter-measures. They're customising and encoding closed circuit control procedures. They're installing emergency pass-codes with instant voice-recognition based on individualised idiolects. By tactical inputting tinkering targeting trialling

They're cleaning out stables excising dead wood pulling up cancerous weeds grafting on new heads. They're cleaning up their acts cracking down on dross and wastage jettisoning excess cargo dumping their shit somewhere else. They're making a clean sweep starting out from scratch clearing all the decks pressing the delete keys. They're actioning proactive initiatives upfronting transparent policy mechanisms keeping the playing fields level and putting new goal posts in place.

They're schematising creative launches ripostes campaigns offensives. In view of futures options exchange-rate-flows and derivatives. They're tunnelling current currencies to meet virtual challenges. They're prioritising and brainstorming and consciousness-raising and snowflaking and streamlining. To implement short-term feasibility studies or interim tactical mergers or ongoing strategic partnerships or long-term take-overs. They're styling and selling and spieling and sealing deals.

Yes, they're really getting somewhere it's got to be important. Maybe they're abolishing pain suffering history death. Or, rat-arsed or stoned or high or zonked out of their minds with boredom, they're doodling in the next room with their Windows˙ games or drooling over new scanners. Or databases spreadsheets software shredders or simulators. Or video- or tele-conferencing with partners in Taipei or Tokyo. Or Thai or Tamil Tigers. Or cruising or scouting or scrying or surfing

Celestial superhighways for Sydney's bounciest beach boys. Or duologuing one-on-one with a call-girl in the Philippines. Or Philadelphia. Or Bombay or Budapest. Or Zagreb or Zimbabwe. Or fiddling with their floppies and anti-virus tools. Or perhaps they're shitting streams or retching out their guts in air-conditioned loos. Or recovering from milder spasms after the canapés prawn cocktails and syllabub. Or from mixing the buffet bubbly with sour South African Sauvignon.

Or from burping or hiccoughs brought on by too many black morning coffees. After delivering face-to-facers at some international meet. Where – despite divorce-proceedings and settlements and decrees nisi and absolute, despite threats from ex-wives letters from solicitors demands from CSA's, despite asthma labyrinthitis herpes and HIV, despite psoriasis piles prostatitis and ME – everything everyone says or does is *Wow Cool Great Fantastic.*

Thus, I hear my smoothest voice slide seamless into fifth gear. Into Informal Insistence Mode. Into offhand downhill preambling and stylishly flattened freewheeling. Into upbeat typecast Yah-speak. Stacked neat and compact with qualifiers and intensifiers. Each syllable understated yet honed for hard, fast delivery. Though ever ready for a backhand volley to riposte my smack-on serve. Like I'd *Be Awfully Grateful If You Wouldn't Mind Trying To Locate Him. It's Actually Rather Important.*

But by land-line or mobile, by cable or satellite, by handset or loudspeaker, by videophone or modem, however I persist, my inflections bear no fruit, my modulations evaporate, my subtle alternations between downright matter-of-factness and delicate sugared politeness remain backgrounded, shadowed, I want just to crawl away in unheralded surrender, hide myself in the loo with a furtive filter tip, dissolve forever, unnoticed. And my attempts to avail myself of latest on-line facilities,

Whether state-of-the art or on the cutting edge, or even merely upgraded from last year's model or module, deactivate on impact, deconstruct on contact, decompress *in vacuo*, disintegrate to zilch. And whoever I do get through to regrets with deep-dish crisp satisfaction, *I'd really like to help but regrettably we are not permitted to divulge information pertaining to associates or personnel to any unauthorised persons. Sorry – it's just one of our in-house rules.*

Eighty-Seven

A hidden agenda. Not mine or yours, in our betrayals of each other. Nor in what pains we caused, and each blamed clean away. Nor griefs or guilts we piled, alternately, on each other. But written into the core. Wrapped, encoded, fastened, into the strings of things themselves.

For what we thought we did, most surely, we did not. Even if we *were* doing the whatever-was-or-seemed. And however in part or perfection, we believed we achieved or failed, really. Yet always something else we could not even in dreams have entertained or envisaged

Lay just outside our grasp, ken, earshot, reckoning. Attacked us from directions we never considered glancing in. Knocked or bowled us over. Grabbed us by the nearest of our most vulnerable extremities. And so, in the thought, deepest, in the doing of the thinking, we eluded

Or deluded most of all ourselves. A joke with no punch-line spat on us, we were its moist squib. It was a dream and was not, both dream and not at once. And though we are not laughing now, each one of us is dunce. And it is oh that immeasurable something I most would treasure now

Which still and forever jiggles, wiggles, wobbles – away, away. Indeed now most of all, when I see so it has done always – burning, assaulting, amazing. With its all-inclusive kit of shocks and innuendoes, packaged without instructions. Or if there is a set, they're written in Janglish, useless.

Speaking of pasts, it is always Poor-Paltry-Gone. Then late, too late, we prophesy and foresee. And speaking of futures, fabricate history. It is the downright elseness in ourselves and all around deceives us, damned crookedness in straightness and vice-versa. Oh Slattern of a Pattern,

Comptroller and Contortioner. Whore named *More*. Bond of *Beyond*. Father alias *Further*. Whatever we know, we do not, and spin and whirl in pain. We lose the single thread, then find and lose again. This is both plan and error, purposelessness and terror. Beneath beseeching clarities

Of what we see as day, semi-conscious or dozing, we take and lay the blame. With infinite excuses, we whistle doubt away. We suffer, interpret, we offer deeds and pray. We mumble, gamble, raise the stakes and play. We cast our silly choices, throw our dice and pay. All of us, always, pay.

Eighty-Eight

When did I last see myself? Myself, did I say? Last night I looked in the mirror and saw a slice of cardboard. Cartoon eyes painted in, and all proper features. Looking really natural. Really relaxed. And on its forehead, printed in shiny letters, like a tattoo: I AM.

You hyped up hypocrite, I laughed, hiding behind appearances, conveniently screened. Who in hell d'you think you are? Come out. Show yourself. I mean reveal yourself really. And the image bared teeth to reply: Look, I'm the one who's not here. I'm

The damn trick of light. Like the rainbow. I'm the retinal illusion. I don't even exist. I'm just the ruddy enantiomorph. Like every time you drop by I'm 100% available. Whenever you deign me a glance. Good Ole Fratello Giordano. Delighted to oblige. At your humble service.

Will you get a load of this creep? sneered the image. You'd make my heart bleed if I had one. If I were real like you. Gee babe I really need you I'm totally hung up on you I depend on you completely I just can't get along without you Brother and suchlike and so-forth.

What a barrel of crap. Why don't you just stop asking questions and start meaning instead? The central problem (i.e. thinking) is thinking there's a central problem. A bull's eye to score fifty smack in the centre of the onion. Plus a super consolation prize to whoever

Can write a dissertation on The Underlying Reality of Bullshit. You think you're so ironic, don't you. And that being sincerely unironic's the answer. I tell you the real problem is you're not ironic *enough*. Not by a long chalk. It isn't because you hate yourself.

It's just that you don't enjoy it. You don't hate yourself *hard* enough. Nor have you even commenced a properly formulated and codified algorithmic series of investigations into The Logocentric Tradition and Its Viability and Implications Within the Current

Comparatively Defined Sociopolitical Ethnomorphic Blah Blah Context. Naturally taking into full account all aspects of potential for discrete and apparently random elements to cohere or at least adhere into a *bricolage* revealing to one and all and sundry

A pattern readily discernible in terms of a developmental that is ahem diachronic connectivity. Which is to say, operating within the Well Established And Christ Almighty Must-We-Go-On-Like-This Time-Honoured Tradition Which Insists You Have To Have A Story

In order to function at all. Time, Buddy Boy, you realised, a story is a fiction and life is the story and the story of the life is a fiction of a fiction made by none other than sweet ole you not merely in order to live the damn thing, let alone die it or at least die in it, but

So you can become your own father, i.e. Manager of Your Self. And not the idiot apprentice of His Eminence the Arch-Trickster and Sorcerer Doctor Lord Editor Me – The Ultimate Illusion. I may indeed have been a scholar once but now I'm a right sodding bastard.

So Toodle-oo Ole Beanbag. Just turn round or turn off the light. And leave me right out of it, will you. Look at yourself not me. Inherit your own damn fatherdom. Sure I'm the subtlest of liars. But mirrors do not deceive. Except to the blind or the dead.

Eighty-Nine

Auntie Mimi has died leaving a full freezer. Frozen bones for stock. Stews for a rainy day. Half a kilo of homemade meatballs flavoured with oregano. Her favourite apple pie, heavily spiced with cloves.

And we who have inherited, what should we do with this goodness? Sling it away, waste it? Bury it all with her? Or eat it, remembering her, since she with her love prepared it?

Five white cut loaves. Two mini-baguettes. Boiled gefilte fish. Hunk of salt beef. Unused packets of crumpets. Dried filo pastry. An opened bag of prawns – oy oy. Peas. Beans. Sweetcorn.

Come, let us feast together, family and friends. For what we are about to receive, may the Lord make us jewly thankful. *Baruch ata Adonai, Elohanu melech ha'olom, ha'motsi lechem min ha aretz.*

Ninety

Oh my cousin, my sister, my unregistered beloved. In a future already made perfect, whose grammar of hope or longing belongs to the present tense. Yet which is not of this time, but presence rendered eternal,

On the threshold of timelessness, in the unsayable margin of death, when I shall be virgin again, at that instant when I approach inexorable completion, and the absolute purity of final, unfettered silence,

I see you stand waiting for me. And on that day, when all darkness is shedded, folding in upon itself, and closing like a book, which no longer contains me, or my name, or my aspirations, or my too weak any words,

It is already printed that you reveal | are-revealing | have-revealed | will-reveal | will-have-revealed | will-have-been-revealing | all mysteries unknown. And unknot all threads. And clarify all confusions.

In the universal grammar you are my enantiomorph. In the yawning of this aeon, I scry you through the evening light aslant over our hillsides. Among primroses and daffodils marshalled in suburban gardens,

I hunger for the touch of your eyes kind and warm upon me. Oh beloved, my sister, my cousin, when I come, knocking upon that door, open to me, I entreat you. Do not turn away from me. Do not ignore me.

Ninety-one

Closed the front door quietly and left the car in the garage for once. Sang all the way to the bridge and continued up Atlanta Road singing. For me a longish walk. Past Prout's the Newsagents

Ali Baba's Kebab House and Chunky Chicken Takeaways. Past A1 Panther Motor Mart Joytime TV Rentals and The Little Drip DIY Superstore. Past Unity Trustee Bank Inc and Unisex Klip n Kurl.

Past Hideout Leather and Hi Fi Video Ultrawave. Past Slink (Leisureline Gowns Ltd) and Regina Hotel With Annexe. Past our only real rivals Safegard Trust Assurance and Loans & Loss Adjusters.

Past the Aquarium Bookshop with Vegan Cafe Upstairs. Past Sheppard Woolf & Crook Estate Agents and the New Beijing Restaurant. Past the Zion Revisionist Chapel and The Ace of Spades.

Queued in the Post Office and Newsagent's behind seven grey haired ladies. All chatting coated buttoned and topped in hats and smiling. And standing there thought, I will not project my condition

On elsewhere and call it England again. Or Garden or Orchard or History or Purgatory or God. This is my city. This my place of belonging. I must make it liveable. This is where I live and work.

And paid for my first-class stamp. And posted my letter still singing. Turned left to go back home and found myself in Hope Street. Familiar terraced houses transformed in late March sun

To yachts lined along a harbourfront waiting to set sail. Dear Rex, I hereby resign, blandly my letter stated. Considering mass unemployment deflation recession etc. And reservoirs of untapped fresh talent

Pouring out of Depts of Bus Admin. Am sure you will have no difficulty in finding a replacement as Floating Manager for all branches within our area of Mddx. In yr rapidly expanding ongoing Prospect subsidiary

Market Advice Planning for Living And Necessity (MAPLAN). To handle both bonds and gilt holdings. Guaranteeing clients' confidence. With Verve. Flare. Enthusiasm. Good Prospects of Early Promotion.

Ninety-Two

I cannot make it cohere is what the old man said. Try though he did through his art. Willing that bridges be built where none had ever existed.

And looked through his eyes' windows. And saw the blue flash of kingfishers. And the moment *benedetto*. And before he went back into silence

Answered himself thus: The light sings eternal . . . i.e. it coheres all right. Even if my notes do not cohere . . . Aye old man, through thick and thin, the world

Sticks together right loyally. Just as it did for our dead we bear within us when alive. And for their dead before them, back to amoebae, to baryons

And though it cares nothing for us whether we're in it on not, and though we forget our mothers and fathers, and shall also be forgotten, and though all things change

Into their opposites – the unknown to the known, the remembered to the forgotten – and merge again into silence from which all may re-emerge. Although pain be endless

This seedling on my windowsill turns constantly towards the light. Its green moment is blessed. And weightless the light's true quality. There is order in being.

I wish I could grasp it forever, this glory the real world inflects. I lose it then find it then lose it. It will not come ever again like this. Ever.

Ninety-Three

To be not here, or anywhere. Simply not to be here. How inconceivable and how terrifying. And how very weird and strange. To disappear, like parents, from presence. Even indeed from memory.

To dissolve, like a word unspoken. To be not even a word upon an unknown tongue. Nor name buried on a lost list in an indecipherable document. Mouldering in an archive or oblivious bureau or vault

And to be wholly untraceable by caretakers or curators. By registrars or attorneys. By neighbours or police. To be unetched in stone. With no wind-sanded serifs blurred and browned by mosses.

To create not a blip, nor quavering pause for half-thought, nor mildest interruption in cordial conversation. To elicit not a yawn from schoolchildren. Nor cool neutral stare from glazed eyes of dancers.

To be not a vanishing wave, or surf upon a wave. Or even ripple of wind grazing surf upon a wave. To be unuttered, unmuttered, unburbled, unwhispered, unbreathed. As these trees will turn

To coal or ash, and all our insects die, well before this winter – moths, midges and mosquitoes, flies, butterflies, daddy-long-legs – so for us will come a winter from which there will be no reawakening.

Nor, my sweetest honeydew, youngest of my children, and most delightful darling of all my dearest darlings, shall we have the compensation of finally being frozen, like primeval bees, in amber.

Ninety-Four

One street on my citymap always eludes me. Though it lies in a zone I know. Between avenues lined with plane trees. At a house in that street I have to deliver a package. A box that rocks and rattles. Wrapped in glossy brown. Sealed with red wax and string.

In heavy hooting traffic. Through slow afternoon heat. Sweating and smoking. I drive back and forth hours. Hunting for the turning, I scan the whole area. Now I think I remember. This must be the one. Hadn't noticed before. Shape of those roofs. That oak tree.

Here as a child I played. On this corner lived bears. And in that house wolves and jackals. When I rode my bike past, very fast, I heard them coming after me. Catch Snatch Dispatch, they spat. But they couldn't get me. Ever. I was always too quick. Or hid.

Hope Street. No Entry. I don't recall that. The names must have changed. I wind my window down and ask a black-scarved widow. Who stares as if through me, then answers in strange dialect: Aye this here beem place you'm lookin fur boy. Do I know

That face. Have I seen those eyes in dreams. Hiding my shudder I thank her. Park and walk away, packet tucked under my arm. At last I find the number. I jerk the rusted bellpull. Paint peels from the door. Again I pull. Again. The bell jangles and jangles.

Hinges creak open on an old man, half shadowed. His eyes gleam pitchblack light. His right arm, wedged behind, slowly edges forward. I offer him my delivery. His wafer smile thickens, like longing. Like a slender knot of welcome. Like a pool of wet red wax

Around a candle base. I am wrapped and tied in his smile, which threatens to throttle and gag me. I break its grip. Look down. In his right arm squats a skull. His left hand grabs my package. He thrusts me his burden instead. In his red toothless laugh

I glimpse a huge blaze. He slams the door in my face. Cradling death upturned in my arms, I stand on the doorstep, shivering. And know this vessel my Grail, my singing immortal head. Now blessèd I back-walk up Hope Street, alive. My cup runneth over.

Ninety-Five

In the parks and among the flowering gardens. My cousin, my sister. At this moment when the conductor of the big brass band rests his baton. At this pause

Steeped in quietness. At this very still point – which is yet not yet an ending – I pray do not come yet. For I am by no means ready. I still have things to do.

For example, to call, to bear witness. To this sweet, sultry, old-new spring, now on the lilac-perfumed brink of spilling into summer. And

To note how cunningly mingled are the stars above with cloud. Cirrus, cumulus, altostratus. Trout-speckled, mackerelled, frog-skinned. Streaked with slime, silver, promises

And countless other etceteras. So, cousin, I must beg your forgiveness. How can I not be besotted with these movements of light and shadow, these

Subtly flickering interplays, these textural incongruities, this chaos of fusings, branchings, connections, intersections? For it is the ordinary spaces

Most call us out to be loved. And the common imperfections that most shape surprise and miracle. And the typical idiosyncrasies that well up

Depths and desires. And by solo and chorus, repeatedly demand that we, who are growing old, once more gaze childlike through them. And each and every time, gaze, as though

For the very first time. Ah, my sister. In the parks and among the flowering gardens. Even when we have crossed over, and are fully bereft of futurity, when shall we

Ever be ready? And even in that split instant, when the soul is in neither zone, neither here nor there, but hovers between, like a butterfly – *shall we ever be ready?*

Ninety-Six

This is a petition. I aim to collect signatures. Hey you out there, are you listening. I want to appeal now. Not only our pasts and futures, but this presence is indiscernible. We peep at it like toddlers playing peekaboo

With parents from behind familiar curtains. Yet the light In here inheres. It is glued to all things everywhere. Nothing in or under it can ever come unstuck. And all things live this light. If only we could bear

The pressure of its weightlessness, meshed texture of its invisibility, bright burden of its burning, that in its openings seals, and in its closures reveals, and in its woundings heals whatever it touches – i.e. *everything*

We might have the singular grace to call this Glory. And by its chords, even be called back to beauty. For how could it have been doubted that joy is our core of being. And this undying light

The grammar underlying our world's common parlances, never pushed by need but being itself velocity, both slow and sudden dawning. So we, by dowsing, through air, invisible threads of light,

Might rediscover the heart's well, once-upon-a-time called Meaning. And be turned, returned, retuned. Like bathing in fresh forest water. Untreated chemically, completely unpolluted. Where trees

Form latticed temples. And branches architraves. And the light shining on, through, across them, particle or wave, makes *music*. We've got a whole movement going. Got ourselves organised.

Led by a great new team. Completely made up of unpaid volunteers. Including children and teenagers. Take out a subscription this week. Join us. Do. Now. The situation is desperate.

Ninety-Seven

Do not approach. Not yet. I am still actively waiting for a call on the other line. I cannot be disturbed. I shan't be back till later. I've several

More trips planned in most intricate detail. I'm in another room, yes, far away on business. And still exceedingly youthful, versatile and hale.

From your implacable heights, turn your still gaze upon the wise. Upon those who have prepared. Upon those who have atoned and forgiven

And been forgiven and shriven. Upon your saints, heroes and martyrs. If there still be any such. Go, swivel your beacon from me. Trill

Elsewhere for the drowning. For those floundering on reefs, those self-buried in sand, those swallowed by the sea's lips, and those

Already in the belly of the cancerous destroyer. I declare myself unpruned, not docked for final judgement. For I have scarcely set out.

Have far too much yet to do. Have not proved myself, even anything. And have not surrendered – nor shall abandon – History.

Ninety-Eight

The aeon lies torn in pieces but you shall mend it with me. With the slow patience of mothers. Who patch one threadbare garment

As a gift for a village child. Who may or may not be born. Who may not live at all. And, from such a Christmas as this, may even not survive.

What else is there to do? Play the Stock Exchange? Now I pay off my debts before I abandon money to the ghosts around the corner

Who, flushed in desirable residences at the smarter end of town, crease themselves in sneers at whatever does not fit them. Their one problem is

Life can never fit them. They fold and unfold their days. Invest them and insure them. But how long ago did they abandon longing.

On the corner, the little prostitutes have just stopped playing Hopscotch. Evening, and for them, time to get down to work.

Oh my sweet Sheba and my more than royal Jonathan, the history of humanity hasn't even started. *Da da, stari moj. Sigurno biće bolje.*

Jer dobro ti znaš, sve je moguće. It is a patchwork quilt, being stitched together in beauty. A coat of many colours. Life, my veil of splendour.

Ninety-Nine

I've been trying to get through for ages but your line was engaged. And you know I can't say a word into an answering machine.

My voice dries up. There has to be somebody real on the other end of the line. No, anybody won't do at all. It's you I wanted to speak to

So I've gone on trying till now. One has to go on trying. No it's not the past I'm talking about. I'm trying to talk about love.

One Hundred

You who sit waiting for me at the other end of my story. At its dead end. In the No-More space. Down the long corridor where your unnumbered room

Has a sign on its door that reads *Nowhere*. Neatly painted in a strange script I can only just decipher. At an address I thought I had lost

Which has just turned up again. Scribbled on a scrap in the pocket of a dusty jacket. One that no longer fits me. That I haven't worn for years.

Who are you, out there? I cannot scry your features. But how infinite your patience. And how replete in acceptance your interiorised smile.

Child of all our futures. Parent of our all pasts. Singularity of singularities. All I know is this. *Volim te puno puno. Mnogo mi nedostaješ.*

Noon. A sky of jade. Below the No-Entry sign from Atlanta Road into Hope Street

Squats a three year old girl. Inspecting moss and grass blades between two slabs in the pavement.

Her left thumb is in her mouth. Her right hand strokes green weeds. Two yards away a boy, her elder brother, maybe,

Scrawls on concrete with a blunt stick. As though writing in code. The girl takes her thumb from her mouth.

Mimi, *she says.* Mi mi. *The boy drops his stick. Stands up.* Yoshi, *he replies.* Yo shi.

Postscript

Among plural narratives a poem's singularity relies on contexts. Its tissues, textures, intermeshings and codings are not only its own. I follow Octavio Paz in believing that 'for the first time in our history, we are contemporaries of all humanity.'[1] Such a belief postulates an enlightened and magnanimous universalism that is threaded in impassioned love for minute particulars. While firmly rooted in modernism and fully acknowledging the achievements of the modernist masters, such a belief can no longer make concessions to the canny and clannish exclusiveness of traditional modernist and neo-modernist avant-gardes. A poem should be to mean as well as mean to be.[2]

The Manager is a poem that consists of one hundred sections and three buffer pieces. It is written in a form that I call the verse-paragraph. This is related to the verset of French poetry, and is used in other European literatures as well. But I have applied and developed this in my own way. I believe it to be a prosodic unit of great strength and flexibility, well suited both to the cadences and varied registers of modern English and to the particular demands made by a long poem.

---

[1] See Octavio Paz, *The Labyrinth of Solitude* (*El Laberinto de la Soledad*), tr. Lysander Kemp, Allen Lane, The Penguin Press, London, 1961, p.162. See also the epigraph to 'Avebury' in *For the Living*, Shearsman Books, Exeter, 2011, p.23.
[2] See Archibald Macleish, 'Ars Poetica'. 1926: 'A poem should not mean / But be'.

The Manager was written between 1978 and 2000. Composition started and ended in Cambridge. I also worked on the book in Belgrade, Dolní Kazimierz, Maribor, Prague, Riga, South Bend, Split, Teneriffe, Teplice, Ustí-nad-Labem, Volos, Warsaw, Washington DC and other places. This second edition contains expanded notes on contexts, sources and references.

The new page format introduced in the second edition of 2008 involved some alterations to the ordering of sections as well as to the text and its patternings, including typography. Further similar changes have been made in this third edition. Some degree of indeterminacy was built into the making of the poem in any case. Of course, all the editions present the same poem.

RB
CAMBRIDGE
2000, 2008 & 2011

Notes

p. 8, section 2
'Songs of Praise': BBC religious TV programme, broadcast every Sunday in the UK. 'Oh-Isn't-He-A-Bit-Like-You-And-Me': line from 'Nowhere Man', a 1960s Beatles song. 'The World About Us': BBC TV documentary.

p. 12, section 6
'Lothlórien': forest realm of the elves in J. R. R. Tolkien's *The Lord of the Rings*. 'Baba': a reference to either or both Indian gurus, Sai Baba of Shirdi and Sathya Sai Baba.

p. 17, section 9
'W. Ken': West Kensington.

p. 23, section 13
'Make Me Feel So Young': Frank Sinatra song.

pp. 24–25, section 14
'The World Is Mine Tonight': lyric by Holt Marvell, music by George Posford. 'Donna Day . . . Lady Summer': transversion of names of singers Lady Day (Billie Holliday) and Donna Summer. 'Before This Night Is Over': reference to lyric by Bryan Adams. 'How the waste remains and kills': villanelle 'Missing Dates' by William Empson: 'It is the waste, the waste remains and kills.'

p. 26, section 15
'knocking on heaven's door': Bob Dylan song.

p. 27, section 16
'Twin Com': twin-engined Comanche. 'Beech': Beechcraft. 'The Needles': rocks in the English Channel. 'Ortac': islet in the Alderney group.

pp. 28–29, section 17
'*Ring a Ring o' Roses*', English nursery rhyme. '*When Sally was a Baby*', English girls' clapping song. 'Oh Sir No Sir No Sir No': chorus of English folk song.

p. 34, section 22
'The Gods': Upper Dress Circle. 'How/Are the mighty fallen': David's lament for Jonathan, 1 *Kings* 1:27.

p. 36, section 23
'Harvest': beer (bitter). 'Hound Dog': Elvis Presley song.

p. 38, section 24
'*huiles* and *crèmes*' (French): oils and creams.

p. 44, section 29
'*Draga*' (Serbian & Croatian): Dear, Darling.

p. 46, section 30
'*Homo aspirans*' (Latin): 'aspiring / aspirating / assisting / breathing / exhaling' Man – as distinct from *Homo sapiens*: 'discreet / judicious / knowing / sensible / well acquainted with the true value of things / wise' man.

pp. 48–49, section 31
'Hack-Up-Your-Doubles-In-An-Old-Bitch-Hag': refers to 'Pack up your troubles in an old kit bag', an English marching song from the First World War. The last four lines refer to and comment on various passages in T. S. Eliot's *The Waste Land*: III: 308 & 311 and V: 373–375.

pp. 52–53, section 34
'His Irish Eyes Aren't Smiling': a reference to 'When Irish eyes are smiling', the lyric by C. Olcott and G. Graff, set to music by Ernest Ball in 1912. 'It's A Long Long Time From May To September': from 'September Song' by Kurt Weill and M. Anderson, made famous by Frank Sinatra. '*Nella profondità del mio cuor io appartengo a voi due*' (Italian): In the depth of my heart I belong to both of you. '*Duende*' (Spanish): term used by Lorca to denote a fiery, passionate quality in art; literally: imp, goblin. 'And the leaves dwindle down': another line from 'September Song' (Kurt Weill & M. Anderson).

p. 61, section 38
The last line embeds a distant echo of Dory Previn's song 'Lemon Haired Ladies': 'go away / no / come back / come back / go away / come back / go away.'

p. 62, section 39
'Manoula' (Greek): little mother, frequent address to a female interlocutor in the rebétika song tradition.

p. 63, section 40
'O thou who chariotest to their dark wintry bed / The wingèd seeds. Where they lie cold. And Lola': see Percy Bysshe Shelley, 'Ode to the West Wind'. 'Rondinella' (Italian): Little swallow. 'Ashes and Sparks. My words among mankind': again, see Shelley's 'Ode to the West Wind'.

pp. 64–65, section 41
'Bête grise and eminence noire': literally, Grey beast and black eminence – a transversion of the epithets 'Eminence grise', i. e. power behind the throne (applied to Cardinal Richelieu), and 'bête noire', i.e. particular object of approbation. 'Ford Open': British prison known for its relatively lax regime and, at one time, high-profile inmates.

pp. 72–73, section 45
'Piero il poverone' (Italian): Peter-Poor-Fellow, poor old Peter. 'Bandito abbandonato' (Italian): Abandoned bandit. 'Ful fetis': echo of the portrait of the Prioresse in Geoffrey Chaucer's 'Prologue' to *The Canterbury Tales*. 'Grazie alla bell' Eleanora' (Italian): Thanks to the lovely Eleanor. 'Everich': every. 'Yche': each. 'Hir': her. 'Hic iacet' (Latin): Here lies. A distant echo is implied of the memorial on King Arthur's tomb in Sir Thomas Mallory's *Le Morte D'Arthur*, '*Hic iacet Arturus, rex quondam, rexque futurus*' ('Here lies Arthur, once and future king'). 'Adam Kadmon': Kabbalistic title for the first man, conceived as a representation or microcosm of the power of the entire universe. 'I very much doubt whether it will ever be me': remote echoes of T. S. Eliot's 'Prufrock'.

p. 74, section 46
'syrtaki' (modern Greek): a contemporary folk-dance. 'To Fengari' (modern Greek): The Moon. Political slogans – 'Avanti il Popolo' (Italian): Forward the People. 'Ελευθερία η θάνατος.'(mod. Greek): Freedom or Death. 'Братство и јединство.' (Serbian): Brotherhood and Unity. 'Brûler Les Écoles. À bas le savoir bourgeois' (French): Burn the Schools. Down with Bourgeois Knowledge.

pp. 76–77, section 47
'Adam Kadmon': see note for pp. 72–73, section 45 above. 'Take a butchers': take a peek. 'One arm bandit': half-Nelson arm lock.

p. 77, section 48
Privilege-loaded British schoolboy slang: 'bags me', it's mine, let it be reserved for me; 'snitch', eavesdrop; 'KV', lookout; 'fains', a warding-off expression – let it not be me or involve me.

p. 80, section 50
'Le Quattro Stagioni' (Italian): The Four Seasons.

pp. 83–84, *Curriculum Vitae*
'Vlet', 'Yildrith', 'Bellona', 'Ashima Slade': these and other names in this section are borrowed from Samuel R. Delaney's science fiction novels. Greek terms and names include: 'baghlamà', musical instrument, a small bouzouki; 'Bellou', 'Vamvakaris' – Sotiria Bellou and Markos Bambakaris, exponents of the rebétika tradition; 'tsiftetéli', a contemporary folk-dance; 'Koré', maiden; 'Horo', Dance.

p. 88, section 53
'Never upon This World had I known life had unleashed so many' echoes T. S. Eliot's *The Waste Land* (I: 62): 'I had not thought death had undone so many'. Eliot's line is a rendering of Dante (*Inferno* 3: 55–57): 'e dietro le venìa sì lunga tratta / di gente, ch'io non averei creduto / che morte tanta n'avesse disfatta.' I can't help wondering if Eliot used the translation by Charles Eliot Norton: '[B]ehind it came so long a train of folk, that I should never have believed death had undone so many'. *The Divine Comedy of Dante Alighieri*, tr. Charles Eliot Norton, Houghton, Mifflin & Co, Boston, 1902, p. 18.

pp. 90–91, section 54
Alcoholic drinks – 'Becherovka' (Czech), fiery aperitif / liqueur named after its creator, Jan Becher. Red Label, a brand of whisky. 'Żubrówka' (Polish), bison-grass vodka. 'Borovička' (Slovak), bilberry gin. 'Lozovača' (Balkan): grape brandy. 'Spasibo Tovarish' (Russian): Thank you Comrade. 'Sondruhu můj' (Czech), My comrade. 'Drahoušku můj štestí moje srdíčko moje milačku můj' (Czech), My darling my happiness my little heart my love. 'Silhouetted against the bedside lamp, the nipples on her long breasts spread out in glowing points.' See T. S. Eliot, *The Waste Land*, II: 108–110: 'Under the firelight, under the brush, her hair / Spread out in fiery points / Glowed into words, then would be savagely still.'

p. 92, section 55
'Thatchers. The Whitehouses and Whitelaws': Margaret Thatcher, Conservative politician, British Prime-Minister, 1979–1990; Mary Whitehouse (1910–2001), British campaigner for morality and decency,

and opponent of the liberalisation of sexual laws; and William Whitelaw (1918–1999) hard-line British Home Secretary, Deputy Prime Minister and Leader of the House of Lords in Margaret Thatcher's government.

p. 97, section 56
CBI: Confederation of British Industry. 'Bishop's Avenue', Hampstead Garden Suburb, North West London: spacious houses for the wealthy.

p. 98, section 59
I had the death of Osip Mandelstam in mind when writing this.

p. 103, section 64
'Some Enchanted Evening': song from the Rodgers and Hammerstein musical, *South Pacific*.

p. 106, section 67
'AWOL': Absent Without Leave.

pp. 108–109, section 68
'Six in the first place', etc: multiple references to the oracular language of *I Ching*, the *Chinese Book of Changes*, version by Richard Wilhelm, tr. Cary F. Baynes, Routledge & Kegan Paul, London, 1960. 'Mann Rogers & Greaves': the pun derives from an anecdote about the Oxford Classics professor, A. C. Clark. While visiting a college farm, Clark saw a bull servicing a cow and remarked to his companion, a younger classicist: 'Blakeway, *omne animal post coitum triste*. ('Every creature is sad after coitus.') He added: 'There was a firm of solicitors in London called Mann, Rogers, and Greaves.'

pp. 112–113, section 70
'November 5th'. Guy Fawkes' Night or Bonfire Night in England. 'The Stefan Batory': Polish ocean liner, named after the King-Consort of Poland (1776–1786); reference also to the 'Stefan Batory poems' by John Matthias – see his *Northern Summer*, Anvil Press Poetry, London, 1984, pp. 145–157. 'Princess Pocahontas': celebrated native American woman (c. 1595–1617), who married an Englishman, John Rolfe. She is buried in Gravesend, where there is a statue to her.

p. 114, section 71
'Trst': Slovenian name for Trieste.

p. 115, section 72
'The pole across the abyss sags to breaking point in the middle': a reference to *I Ching*, the *Chinese Book of Changes*, Hexagram 28, *Ta Kuo/ Preponderance of the Great*: 'The ridgepole sags to the breaking point.'

See the Richard Wilhelm version, tr. Cary F. Baynes, Routledge & Kegan Paul, London, 1960, pp. 111 ff.

pp. 118–119, section 74
'Adam Kadmon': see the note above to pp. 72–73, Section 45. The phrases 'a loon and malely loitering' and 'Where no birds ding-a-ling' refer to John Keats, 'La Belle Dame Sans Merci': 'O what can ail thee, Knight at Arms, / Alone and palely loitering. / The sedge has withered from the lake, / And no birds sing'. For 'comfort me with flagons' see *The Song of Solomon*, 2:5. 'Nella Capella della Solitudine' (Italian): In the Chapel of Solitude.

p. 120, section 75
'A garden inclosed is my sister': *The Song of Solomon*, 4:12. 'And overhead up grew / Insuperable highth of loftiest shade': John Milton, *Paradise Lost*, 4: 137–138. 'Sleep o gentle sleep': William Shakespeare, 2 *Henry IV*, 3.1:7–10.

p. 122, section 77
'Dunwich', village in Suffolk, once one a large port, much of which was washed away by storms in 1286 and 1328 and gradually lost to the sea by erosion (long shore drift). 'Ys, drowned under salt and foam', cathedral-city buried under the sea in Breton legend, source for: (1) Debussy's piano prelude, *La cathédrale engloutie* ('The Sunken Cathedral'), 1914; (2) Ceri Richards' series of paintings of the same title, 1957–1962, see Mel Gooding, *Ceri Richards*, Cameron & Hollis, Moffatt, 2002, pp. 135–151; and (3) my prose-poem, 'Ys' (early 1970s), in *For the Living*, Shearsman Books, 2011, pp. 97–116. The phrase 'Former Ludoslovakia. Or was it Severoslavia' contains puns based on roots in Serbian/Croatian: *lud*, mad; *severo*, northern – as distinct from *jugo* [pron. yugo], southern.

pp. 124–125, section 78
'A complex can only be really conquered if it's lived out to the full. So you must try to pull it into your centre / And drink it down to the dregs.' See Carl Gustav Jung, 'Psychological Aspects of the Mother Archetype', *The Archetypes and the Collective Unconscious*, Collected Works 9(i), tr. R. F. C. Hull, Routledge & Kegan Paul, London, §. 184, pp. 98–9:

> As we know, a complex can be really overcome only if it is lived out to the full. In other words, if we are to develop further we have to draw to us and drink down to the very dregs what, because of our complexes, we have held at a distance.

'No alternative, do you see, but to face into the dark approaching, unprejudiced and quite innocently, / And find out what its secret aims are and what it holds for you. [. . .] The only cure really is patience.' See M.-L. Von Franz, 'The Process of Individuation' in Carl C. Jung et al., *Man and His Symbols*, Aldus Books, London, 1979. p. 167:

> It is exactly the same in the initial crisis in the life of an individual. One is speaking of something that is impossible to find or about which nothing is known. In such moments all well-meant sensible advice is completely useless – advice that urges one to try to be responsible, to take a holiday, not to work so hard (or to work harder), to have more (or less) human contact, or to take up a hobby. None of that helps, or at least only rarely. There is only one thing that seems to work; and that is to turn directly toward the approaching darkness without prejudice and totally naïvely, and to try to find what its secret aim is and what it wants from you.

p. 129, section 81
'*ūhtcearu*' (Anglo-Saxon): dawn-sorrow.

p. 136, section 86.
'CSA': Child Support Agency.

pp. 140–141, section 88
'Fratello' (Italian): Brother. '*Bricolage*' (French): more or less random collection of objects made into a pattern: a term adopted by some anthropologists and artists.

p. 142, section 89
'Baruch ata Adonai Elohanu melech ha'olom ha'motsi lechem min ha aretz.' (Hebrew): Blessed art thou, O Lord our God, King of the universe, who bringest forth bread from the earth. The blessing before a meal.

p. 143, section 90
'beloved, my sister': *The Song of Solomon*, 4: 9–12 and 5: 1–2. In writing the last lines of this poem I had at the back of my mind the last line of Bob Dylan's song, 'Sara': 'Don't ever leave me, don't ever go.'

p 146, section 92
This section contains multiple echoes and quotations from Ezra Pound's *Drafts and Fragments of Cantos CX–CXVII*, Faber & Faber, London, 1970: (1) 'I cannot make it cohere' – 'Canto CXVI', p. 26; (2) 'And saw the blue flash of kingfishers. And the moment *benedetto*' – 'Notes for

Canto CXII et seq.', 'For the blue flash and the moments / benedetta', p. 31 (benedetto, benedetta, blessed); (3) The light sings eternal' – 'Canto CXV', p. 25; and (4) 'i.e. it coheres all right. Even if my notes do not cohere' – 'Canto CXVI', p. 27. In line 8, in full and proper recognition of the extent of Pound's anti-semitism, I have changed the inappropriate word 'rabbi', which appeared in the first edition, to 'old man'. 'Baryons': particles postulated by physicists to have existed solely during and in the instantaneous wake of the Big Bang.

p. 148, section 94
'His eyes gleam pitchblack light.' See my sequence 'Black Light', *For The Living*, Shearsman Books, Exeter, 2011, especially pp. 153 and 173. For the Grail as severed head / upturned skull, see: (1) Jean Markale, *Women of the Celts*, tr. A. Mygind et al., Gordon Cremonesi, London, 1975, pp. 177–190; (2) numerous drawings and paintings made by Ceri Richards on themes of Dylan Thomas, c. 1953–1956; and (3) my *Keys to Transformation: Ceri Richards and Dylan Thomas*, Enitharmon Press, London, 1981, pp. 53–55 and figs. 17–20, 23 AND 25.

p. 150, section 95
'In the parks and among the flowering gardens.' A (deliberate) mistranslation of the first line of a song by Mikis Theodorakis: 'Sta perivólia mes tous anthisménous kýpous'. 'My cousin my sister': see the note above to p. 154, section 90.

p. 154, section 97
In part, a response to T. S. Eliot's 'The Dry Salvages', the second of his *Four Quartets*.

p. 155, section 98
'Oh my sweet Sheba and my more than royal Jonathan': I *Kings* 10:13 and 2 *Kings* 1. *Da da, stari moj. Sigurno biće bolje. / Jer dobro ti znaš, sve je moguće* (Serbian): Yes yes, my old friend. Things are bound to get better. / Because of course you know – everything's possible. 'A coat of many colours': Jacob's gift to Joseph, *Genesis*, 37:3.

p. 156, section 99
'No it's not the past I'm talking about. I'm trying to talk about love.' Adapted from George Seferis, 'The Thrush' III: 'I'm not talking to you about bygones, I'm talking about love.' See *Collected Poems, 1924–1955*, tr. Edmund Keeley and Philip Sherrard, Jonathan Cape, 1969, pp. 330–331.

p. 157, section 100
'*Volim te puno puno. Mnogo mi nedostaješ.*' (Serbian): I love you lots and lots. Miss you awfully.

www.ingramcontent.com/pod-product-compliance
Lightning Source LLC
Chambersburg PA
CBHW022009160426
43197CB00007B/357